The Educator's
Practical Guide to
EMOTIONAL
INTELLIGENCE

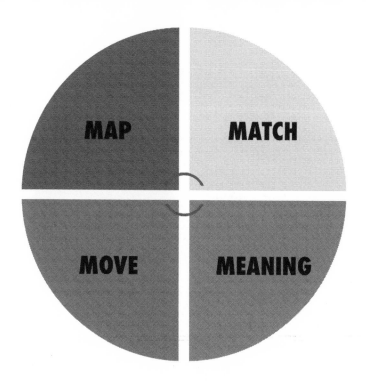

MAP   MATCH

MOVE   MEANING

David R. Caruso PhD   **Lisa T. Rees** MPA   **David Adams** MEd

First published by EI Skills Group in 2020
www.EiTeacher.com
blueprint@EiTeacher.com

ISBN 978-1-945028-31-1

Book design and production by Adam Robinson for GoodBookDevelopers.com

The Educator's Practical Guide to
Emotional Intelligence

David R Caruso, Ph.D.
Lisa T Rees, PCC, MPA
David Adams, M.Ed.

Contents

PREFACE

About Us

We want you to know a little bit about us and why we wrote this book.

David R. Caruso, Ph.D. College was not quite what I expected and I dropped out after two, difficult years. One of the jobs I took, after washing dishes at a local restaurant, was as an orderly in a nursing home. The nursing home had been converted to the care of multiply-handicapped children and adults, the result of deinstitutionalization in the 1970's. As I tried to provide compassionate care to the residents, a sense of powerlessness and despair was overwhelming at times. That's when, as a result of another major initiative called the Education of All Handicapped Children Act, the local school district pulled up a mobile home next to the facility to start a school. A full-time teacher was hired and I became the teacher assistant. For the first time, I felt I was making a positive difference in the lives of people and my work mattered. Thinking I could be of greater help if I had a degree, I returned to college with a sense of purpose and from there went to graduate school. It was in grad school where I met Jack Mayer, one of the developers of the theory of emotional intelligence. A postdoctoral fellowship at Yale followed where I met Peter Salovey, the other developer of the theory. They had met separately and were quite advanced in the work when I joined them in the 1990's; my role being the application of their work to practice. Soon after, I conducted my first EI training workshop for teachers and educators in 2002 when a colleague, Chuck Wolfe, brought me to a school in Connecticut, and then another in Long Island, New York. In that training, I introduced the Mood Meter (Mood Map in this book) and EI Blueprint which have since been taught around the world. By 2004, I was conducting EI training in other schools along with colleague Marc Brackett. This work led to the development of RULER training which Marc and his team have expanded into what it is today. Currently, my time is split between a part-time administrative role at Yale and conducting EI training around the world. I also have a title of research affiliate at the Yale Center for Emotional Intelligence. With Jack Mayer and Peter Salovey, I am the co-author of the Mayer, Salovey, Caruso Emotional Intelligence Test (MSCEIT), the co-author of *The Emotionally Intelligent Manager* (with Peter), and with Marc and Robin Stern I am co-author of the *Anchors of Emotional Intelligence* RULER book. When people ask me how I got into this field, or about my career trajectory or career progression, I usually just smile and shake my head. I really don't know how all this happened, but I am extremely grateful to the people who helped me get here.

Lisa T. Rees, PCC, MPA. I am an experienced leader, coach and instructor with the U.S. Citizenship and Immigration Services (USCIS). Over the last three decades, I led multiple teams for USCIS implementing financial systems and cost efficiencies throughout the agency before switching career fields to become a leadership coach in 2015. I am certified in the MSCEIT, as well as in Appreciative Inquiry (AI) and numerous leadership assessment tools. I wanted to write this book to share the power of emotional intelligence with educators, and because I have a very fond place in my heart for them. Throughout my academic journey, I was fortunate to have teachers who went beyond the curriculum to spark curiosity in me, encourage me when I wanted to give up and opened my mind to a new world. I was brought up by parents who valued education and its importance, and it was because of them I have tremendous respect for educators. Not to mention the fact my father was a teacher and Department Head of Foreign Language for decades. I even had the privilege of having him as my French teacher in high school! Over the years, I saw his commitment to his students and colleagues, the emotional connection he had with them, and the love they showed him years after he retired. For him, like many of his colleagues, teaching came with a toll—burnout, worry, concern, despair—but it also came with great reward, that for him, made it all worthwhile. I hope this book will help educators be the best they can be because we need amazing teachers now more than ever.

David Adams, M.Ed. I am the Director of Social-Emotional Learning at The Urban Assembly. I previously served as the Social-Emotional Learning Coordinator for District 75 in New York City, where I shaped the District's approach to social and emotional development for students with severe cognitive and behavioral challenges. I have worked internationally in schools in England, standing up and evaluating programs of positive behavioral supports and social-emotional learning as a research intern at Yale University's Health, Emotion and Behavior Lab, and published multiple academic papers around the relationship of social-emotional competence, and student academic and behavioral outcomes. I serve on the Board of Directors of CASEL and served on the Council of Distinguished Educators of the Aspen Institute's National Commission of Social, Emotional and Academic Development (NCSEAD). I am also a Civil Affairs Officer in the Army Reserve, classified as an *Expert Functional Skill Practitioner* in Public Education, and hold a M.Ed. in Educational Psychology. I have spent my career in schools, working in special education, general education, charter schools, district schools, in urban, rural and suburban contexts across the country. I've watched the education field shift from small schools, to standards-based reform, to teacher accountability. Nevertheless, one of the enduring lessons I have learned in all this time is students do better in classrooms where teachers care about them, teachers do better in schools where administrators care about them, and schools do better in neighborhoods where people care about each other. Learning the skills of Emotional Intelligence is an integral step in creating a social and emotional environment for student success.

About Our Collaboration

Some years ago when David (Caruso) needed someone to help co-facilitate both MSCEIT and EI training sessions he reviewed the list of hundreds of people who he had trained and came up with one name at the top of the list, Lisa Rees. Lisa has decades of hands-on experience leading people, coaching individuals and making a positive difference in difficult environments. David met Dave Adams at the Yale Center for Emotional Intelligence (although it was called the Health, Emotions, Behavior Lab at the time). They fell out of touch and re-connected, of all places, at an EI conference in Western Australia. Needing an educator co-author for this book David immediately thought of Dave given his experience, education and his desire to be a force for good in the world. The three of us are a new team and it's been a positive and constructive experience. While we have different backgrounds and experiences, we do seem to have a few things in common. The main value driving this book is our desire to repair and improve the world. We sincerely believe and hope this book will help you become a better educator, perhaps to reconnect you with your original motivation to enter the profession, and to give you another set of tools and skills to engage in making the world a better and more just place.

We hope you find value in our book and we thank you for the important work you do,

David R. Caruso, New Haven, Connecticut
Lisa T. Rees, Burlington, Vermont
David Adams, New York City, New York

INTRODUCTION

You entered the field of education to change the world, and change it for the better. You acquired a wide range of skills through formal education, invaluable experience in the classroom, the generosity of mentors and the lessons you learned from students.

There are many ways to teach, and there are many skills and traits successful educators possess. Educators – teachers, aides, principals, superintendents, heads of school – need a vast array of skills to succeed and thrive. Great educators have the ability to accurately read emotions, to harness the power of emotions, to understand the causes of emotions and to effectively manage emotions, both in the context of instruction, and in everyday interactions with students, staff and parents. In other words, they possess a high level of *emotional intelligence*.

There are many books on emotional intelligence and even more on teaching, educational administration and educational effectiveness. They all have important things to offer. ***This book is designed to provide you – in the most efficient way possible – with practical skills and tips to leverage emotions to help you become a more effective educator.*** This is not a general book about teaching, or being an educational administrator per se, or even an overview of emotional intelligence or socio-emotional learning. Rather, it is a book about utilizing the skills of emotional intelligence as an educator. We get right to the point, providing you with practical strategies to leverage your emotional intelligence skills as an educator. Then we provide you with concrete and practical "Blueprints" to help you address the many challenges educators face.

This book is for those who know that being a great educator is about building trust and forging strong relationships that include emotional connections. And yet, as anyone who has sparred with a recalcitrant 10th grader, or tried to decipher the intricacies of social life of a middle schooler knows, this is not as simple as it seems. Emotions are multi-faceted and incredibly complex, and emotional intelligence provides you with a skill set to harness the power of emotions. Students enter your classroom or school filled with emotions and these emotions can facilitate academic and social success, or they can interfere with their learning and development. While emotions help us develop trust, emotions can also derail us from achieving goals. Emotions can energize us, but when not effectively managed, emotions can overwhelm the best of us, even educators—especially when those emotions are unpleasant. This book provides ideas on how to better map and manage emotions in educational settings so you can bring your best self to your classroom and school.

A guiding principle throughout this book is emotions are neither good nor bad, they are information and a source of data. As a result, you will see us embrace *all* emotions rather than simply encouraging the development of happy educators. The emphasis on positive emotions in the last several years may be a reaction to psychology's historical focus on illness; but it may also have gone too far. There are times when anxiety is smart and effective, such as when you are readying yourself for a major presentation to the school board. There are times when anger is justified, such as when we become aware of injustice, bias and racism[1]. Inequities in educational systems *should* anger us, and we should leverage and harness that anger to effect positive, social change. At the same time, we should not interpret this to mean we can be "jerks," treat people poorly or be destructive. The key is to be smart about emotions and being smart about emotions requires a high level of skill; it requires a high level of emotional intelligence.

---

1   We suggest a great book on how positive psychology has gone wrong: Ehrenreich, B. (2009). *Bright-Sided: How Positive Thinking Is Undermining America*. New York: Henry Holt.

By being smart about emotions, and knowing how you and others feel, and whether these emotions are helpful or not, you can leverage the power of emotions to successfully teach, lead, educate and serve others in the classroom and at school. To be clear: sadness, anger and anxiety have tactical, short-term advantages only when in the hands of educators possessing the highest level of emotional intelligence. Otherwise, we risk damaging relationships and adding to inequities in our classrooms and schools.

To be even clearer about this point, the most effective educators are those who create climates of respect, treat people with decency and create a pleasant environment for students, faculty, staff and families.

Emotional Intelligence – Origin and Definition

Emotional intelligence means different things to different people. Emotional intelligence became part of our culture in 1995, when journalist and psychologist Daniel Goleman[2] wrote a book on emotional intelligence that started a worldwide conversation and brought emotional intelligence into the spotlight. As a scientific theory however, emotional intelligence was first written about in a 1990 paper by John "Jack" Mayer and Peter Salovey[3] who defined emotional intelligence as: "The ability to monitor one's own and other's feelings and emotions, to discriminate among them and to use this information to guide one's thinking and action." Jack is now a professor of psychology at the University of New Hampshire and Peter Salovey is the president of Yale University. In their view, emotions can be smart and helpful, and emotional intelligence is a set of "hard" rather than "soft" skills.

In 1996, David Caruso joined Jack and Peter to begin to create an ability-based test, like an IQ test, that measures a person's

---

2   Goleman, D. (1995.) Emotional Intelligence. NY: Bantam Books.

3   Salovey, P. & Mayer, J. D. (1990). Emotional intelligence. Imagination, Cognition, and Personality, 9, 185-211.

ability to perceive, facilitate, understand and manage emotions. They developed one test, and then a few years later created the Mayer, Salovey, Caruso Emotional Intelligence Test (MSCEIT) which measures a person's emotional intelligence and helps them leverage their strengths and become aware of areas they may want to develop[4]. David began to apply the research in many environments, including schools, and developed an emotional intelligence training program for teachers and educational administrators. A colleague, Marc Brackett, attended training sessions and collaborated with David to develop the initial ability-based emotional intelligence training program for educators. This book is based upon the work of Jack and Peter, incorporates research based on the MSCEIT and continues the work we started in schools many years ago.

Why You Might Benefit from This Book

Our book is designed for busy educators who know the importance of emotions in the classroom and schools, and want useful tips on how to strengthen their skills using real life examples. By the end of this book, and with a little practice, you can effectively harness the power of emotions and transition from being a good educator to a great educator.

Many people feel they have a high level of emotional intelligence and may not think they need to develop their skills. Consider research using the MSCEIT where people tended to overestimate their EI. What is concerning about the results of these studies is the more people overestimate their EI, the less likely they are to be interested in developing their skills[5]. Consider for a moment the cost

---

4   Mayer, J., Salovey, P., & Caruso, D. (2002). The Mayer, Salovey Caruso Emotional Intelligence Test. Toronto: MHS.

5   Sheldon, O.J., Dunning, D., & Ames, D.R. (2014). Emotionally unskilled, unaware, and uninterested in learning more: Reactions to feedback about deficits in emotional intelligence. Journal of Applied Psychology, 99, 125-137.

of inaccurately "reading" people. Let's say you perceived a student as being angry when they were actually anxious and worried. Wouldn't you approach this situation differently and wouldn't the outcome of the interaction be vastly different if you had read their emotions more accurately?

The four skills of emotional intelligence seem basic and straight-forward, and it looks easy to leverage these skills in daily situations. Frankly, it's not that difficult, as we all possess these skills to some degree; we must in order to survive, let alone thrive in our challenging world. We can all benefit from strengthening, practicing and honing these skills. The real challenge each of us faces is deploying these skills on a consistent basis, in real-time, at a high level of expertise, and under stressful conditions. We've met only a few people—out of thousands—who can do this. That means most of us can work on developing our emotional intelligence skills!

THE EMOTIONAL INTELLIGENCE FRAMEWORK

The framework of emotional intelligence is simple and contains four abilities – the ability to Perceive, Facilitate, Understand and Manage emotions. Each ability has its own characteristics and all work together to form emotional intelligence. We use the more memorable labels of *Map* (Perceive), *Match* (Facilitate), *Meaning* (Understand) and *Move* (Manage), for better retention[6] , as illustrated in Figure 1.

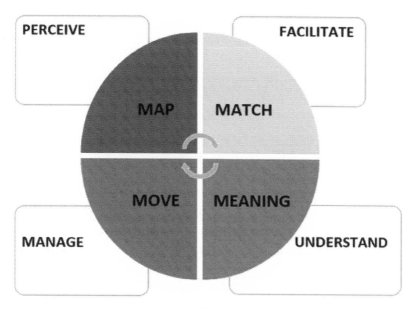

Figure 1: The EI Ability Model

---

6   "Use" is another label for "Facilitation" or "Facilitation of Thought."

Some approaches to EQ include various aspects of personality or temperament such as optimism or assertiveness. Our approach to emotional intelligence—sometimes called the ability model of EI—consists of a set of hard skills or abilities. In this approach, EI is an intelligence, related to other intelligences. There is nothing wrong or unimportant about assertiveness, but it is a traditional personality trait and not a skill, nor part of emotional intelligence, at least in our view.

The 4 M Model, RULER and CASEL

The four hard skills of EI in this book may be familiar to you. They are from the 1997 Mayer-Salovey model of EI and re-labeled in Table 1 to make them a bit more memorable. (The model was updated and revised recently, see Mayer, Caruso & Salovey, 2016).

You might also be familiar with an EI model applied in schools called RULER. RULER is also based on the Mayer-Salovey model, again using different labels. Early training sessions on EI began with a review of basic principles such as confidentiality, experiencing emotions and being able to opt out. These principles became the interactive "Charter." The Mood Meter initially used a 10-point scale and was later revised to a -5 to +5 scale for use in schools. Both the EI Blueprint and Mood Meter (in this book called the Mood Map), were part of our early training and included in a 2004 book (Caruso & Salovey). The Intervening Moment, a classic emotion management strategy, and also used in our early training, became the Meta Moment in RULER training. If you have already done RULER training, this book will support what you've learned! If you are considering RULER training, please do so – you'll receive support and materials to help bring the program to your school.

The Collaborative for Academic, Social, and Emotional Learning (CASEL) has a different model of skills, attitudes and behaviors which are based on the work of Daniel Goleman, who wrote the 1995 book "Emotional Intelligence." The CASEL model includes self-awareness, self-management, social awareness, relationship skills and responsible decision making. While SEL is not the same as EI, they are related, perhaps first or second cousins. EI consists of more basic skills and abilities; whereas SEL includes a broader range of characteristics including, as CASEL notes, attitudes as well as values.

Table 1, along with Figure 1, provides more detail about these approaches and, in our view, how they overlap.

Mayer-Salovey	RULER	CASEL	4 M's
Perceive	Recognize / Express	Self-Awareness Social Awareness	**Map**
Facilitate/Use		Relationship Skills	**Match**
Understand	Understand / Label	Decision Making	**Meaning**
Manage	Regulate	Self- Management Relationship Skills	**Move**

Table 1. Labels for Different EI Abilities

The Case for Emotional Intelligence

Why does emotional intelligence matter for students, educators, schools and families? The research on EI, the ability model, reveals that EI predicts certain outcomes. Summaries of the research on socio-emotional learning can be found at CASEL, and for emotional intelligence, we urge you to review the scientific literature directly[7]. Emotional intelligence matters in schools—students do better academically and socially, and teachers experience less burnout. In a

---

7   See Rivers, S.E., Handley-Miner, I.J., Mayer, J.D. & Caruso, D.R. (2020). Emotional Intelligence. *Cambridge Handbook of Intelligence (2nd ed.)* for a recent summary of research.

recent study of studies, called a meta-analysis[8], Carolyn MacCann and colleagues found that EI, especially EI defined as an ability, predicts academic achievement of school children. Of course, EI is not the most important factor in being a great educator, it is one of many factors. And to be clear, while our book is based on evidence-based practices, the specific practices we list in this book have not been subjected to such analyses.

There have been bold claims that EI can be easily learned (unlike IQ), but they were unsupported. After many years of research, there now exist data suggesting that EI itself – defined and measured as an ability – can be increased. EI programs in schools, especially SEL programs, had been hailed as having an enormous impact on the lives of students. But one question which has taken time to address is whether the effects of SEL programs fade over time, as do many such programs, and frankly, was the expectation of one of the authors (DC). New data reported by CASEL suggest the positive outcomes of SEL programs do indeed last and are sustained over a long period of time. And, that is why we do research—to prove or disprove hypotheses!

But whether actual gains in skills are large or small, in many ways, it really doesn't matter whether EI itself can be increased. Why? Consider this analogy: someone has poor spatial ability and as a result, when traveling to a new location and given a map and directions, gets lost. Can we increase the person's spatial ability? Perhaps. But an easier solution is to provide this individual with a GPS. The result? They don't get lost! An analogy for educators may be a child with a learning difference, where the student's skills result in them skipping lines when reading text, which leads to poor reading comprehension. You can provide the student with reading software which presents text line by line, or for printed matter, a ruler which they move down the page line by line. The result? The student doesn't skip lines and reading comprehension increases dramatically. This

---

8   MacCann, C., Jiang, Y., Brown, L. E. R., Double, K. S., Bucich, M., & Minbashian, A. (2019). Emotional intelligence predicts academic performance: A meta-analysis. *Psychological Bulletin, 146*(2), 150–186.

book provides you with a GPS for emotions and a series of remedial and compensatory emotional intelligence strategies. It's not magic, but you have to work at these skills, apply them intentionally, get feedback, hone the skills and try again.

Cautions When Using Emotional Intelligence

"The function of education is to teach one to think intensively and to think critically. Intelligence plus character – that is the goal of true education."[9] (Dr. Martin Luther King). Our research and observations support the use of emotional intelligence in education. At the same time, we need to make sure we are always looking to improve our understanding and application of emotional intelligence and to be aware of possible misuses of it. We do not want to engage in merely "faith-based" practices and instead, prefer to be skeptical and open-minded. In other words, we wish to think intensively about what we do and not blindly accept assertions about an intervention or program. Along those lines, there are a few cautions about the application of emotional intelligence in education.

Make Sure EI Is a Force for Positive Social Change
When the goal of education is "Intelligence plus character," teachers and educators who score higher in EI experience better outcomes for their students and schools, and people scoring higher in EI create more positive work environments and have better-quality relationships. The outcomes of high EI are mostly for good, but not always. Some people who score high on Move emotions, and are also devious and power-hungry (scoring high on a scale called Machiavellianism), can use their skill as a manipulative tool. The lesson here is to be careful as you develop your EI skills and those of others.

But there is another issue with how EI is deployed in schools. When an adult, administrator or anyone with power asks another

---

9   https://thekingcenter.org/teach-in/

person to share their feelings, to open themselves up, they are implicitly pressuring the other person, the student for example, to share. This means you need to engage these skills with great care and intention. You can't be casual about it and you must not ever use the information gleaned through these skills to harm someone. We are not implying the readers of this book, and people interested in EI and SEL, lack this sort of awareness. It's that all of us, at times, act in ways that are not congruent with our values. Therefore, be careful, be considerate and be thoughtful when using these skills.

Emotional Intelligence and Cultural Competence

Perhaps the main case against using emotional intelligence in a school setting is when teaching EI skills is devoid of cultural competence. CASEL notes, "Cultural competence is the ability to examine the various social and cultural identities of oneself and others, understand and appreciate diversity from a historically grounded and strengths-focused lens, recognize and respond to cultural demands and opportunities and build relationships across cultural backgrounds" (CASEL.org).

Dr. Dena Simmons of the Yale Center for Emotional Intelligence makes a compelling argument for the need for SEL to be taught with awareness of the "larger socio-political context, which is fraught with injustice and inequity, and affects our students' lives.[10]" She continues by noting teaching skills, such as relationship skills, without referring to conflicts resulting from systemic injustice, inequity or racism, shortchanges students at the least. Dealing with these complex issues may make us uncomfortable, and she notes educators require courage to engage in culturally-competent practices. We agree, and we also recognize this lack of comfort is a signal that the topic is important and matters. As we mentioned earlier, a guiding principle throughout this book is emotions are not good, negative,

---

10 www.ascd.org/publications/newsletters/education_update/apr19/vol61/num04/Why_We_Can't_Afford_Whitewashed_Social-Emotional_Learning.aspx

bad or positive; they are tremendously valuable sources of data and information. We recognize different cultural values and norms govern outward displays of emotion and have strived to write a book linking practical strategies with the theoretical basis educators need to develop their approaches to emotional intelligence.

There are several important principles driving this work. First, the ability model is a developmental one, the skills emerge over the course of our development. Second, when you hear someone is or is not emotionally intelligent, that's a misunderstanding of what emotional intelligence is. No one "lacks" emotional intelligence; there are individual differences in levels of EI but it's not a binary choice. Therefore, we all possess these skills and can develop them further. Third, and most important, if you review the ability model framework, cultural competence is embedded within it. For us to accurately perceive the emotions of others we need to be aware of cultural display rules. We need to know, for example, that a student may feel proud of their work but they don't overtly show this because some cultures restrict "the expression of emotions such as pride"[11] We need to know calling on someone in class can be embarrassing to the student. The highly emotionally intelligent educator is sensitive to context and is aware of the cues and ways emotions are expressed, as well as culturally-specific causes of different emotions[12]. Therefore, when using these principles to solve problems, remember culturally competent instructional knowledge and approaches should come first.

Let's Go!

After sharing limitations and cautions about applying emotional intelligence in educational settings, you may be feeling a lower level of energy and a lower level of pleasantness. After all, we turned a

---

11   From an article by V.A. Dzokoto (2018). https://doi.org/10.3389/fpsyg.2018.01916

12   Here we refer you to theories of socially constructed emotion by Jim Averill and Lisa Feldman Barrett.

critical and cautious eye on EI, and you are likely reading this book because of the promise EI holds in creating respectful and effective classrooms and schools. As we hope you will see in the next section of the book, emotions can help us think. This feeling of lower energy and pleasantness focuses your attention on details, helpful when reading a more critical analysis of a field. As we turn to developing and applying the four skills of emotional intelligence, we hope your energy and pleasantness levels will increase as you consider how you can apply these skills. You may become more reflective and perhaps at times, even a bit inspired. That's what emotional intelligence is all about. It's about being able to welcome **all** emotions, integrate and reflect on them, and finally leverage their power to take us to places we never imagined. Developing EI takes skill and practice, and this book will help you become a more emotionally intelligent educator. So, get ready emotionally and let's go!

PART ONE

Building Your Emotional Intelligence Skills

MAP EMOTIONS

Let's begin developing and deploying your emotional intelligence skills. And, we start at the beginning, with Mapping emotions.

Emotions contain data. You make decisions based on data: lesson plans, reports, grades, evaluations, policies, discipline, etc. When was the last time you made an important decision based on emotions? The answer should be "every single time," or perhaps more accurately, "every time I made a <u>good</u> decision." We are taught to keep emotions out of professional decision making, but emotions impact everything we do whether we realize it or not. Sometimes emotions help us make great decisions – if we leverage the skills of EI. But at other times, emotions trip us up because we fail to accurately read the situation.

Think of your typical school day. What emotions do you feel and see? And what impact are these emotions having on your ability to lead, teach and connect with students, teachers and parents? Chances are you experience emotions constantly, but are you paying attention to them? Perhaps you feel emotions aren't relevant in the classroom—but you may want to think again. Take a moment to recall a recent lesson you led where you had a very specific goal in mind. You began the lesson plowing through the material and then something happened. A student became distracted and made a comment. Perhaps they became frustrated and started to raise their voice, or became despondent and started to cry. As a result, you find yourself surprised and confused by their reactions, and the lesson you carefully planned, is now a distant memory. Unfortunately, this happens more than it should. That is why the first part of emotional intelligence is accurately identifying how others are feeling before moving further into the lesson or the discussion.

How do you know how a colleague or student is feeling? Chances are if you asked one of your students how they are feeling they would say something like fine, good or ok. Unfortunately, these answers are not very helpful in accurately identifying someone's emotions. The polite responses, so commonplace in today's society, are almost completely without meaning. In all likelihood, when we ask, "how are you?," we do so to be polite, not to get an honest answer! Sheryl Sandberg, in her book written with Adam Grant, *Option B[13]*, tells the story of how people asked, "how are you?" right after her husband died, and how they likely expected the typical non-answer.

One way to really know how someone is feeling is by using the Mood Map (Figure 2)[14]. Emotions can be measured on two axes – by their level of energy and their level of pleasantness. (The four quadrants are typically printed in color and we refer to each Mood Map quadrant by their color.) If someone has high energy and high pleasantness, most likely they are feeling happiness and joy (the Yellow quadrant). If they are experiencing high energy and low pleasantness, then chances are they are feeling angry, frustrated or overwhelmed (the Red quadrant). If they are feeling low energy and low pleasantness, then they may be experiencing boredom or sadness (the Blue quadrant). And finally, if they are experiencing low energy and high pleasantness, they are most likely feeling satisfied and content (the Green quadrant).

A small but important point about feelings and how we talk about them; we prefer the term *pleasantness* to refer to our feelings rather than saying they are negative or positive. It sends a message

---

13   Sandberg, S. & Grant, A. (2017). *Option B*. NY: Knopf. They cite David Caruso in their book.

14   You may be familiar with the Mood Meter. David (C) first started using it in the early 2000's and it was adopted by the RULER program.

that how we feel is important and even unpleasant, or what many people call negative emotions, have a role in our lives. We'll discuss this in more detail later in the book.

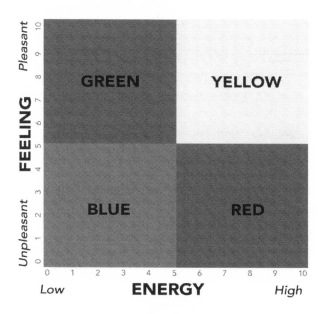

Figure 2: The Mood Map

Plotting Your Feelings with the Mood Map

Start with Energy on the x-axis of the Mood Map. How much energy do you have right now, at this moment? If you have as much energy as you have ever had and feel incredibly energetic, then you would be an 8, 9 or 10 on the Energy dimension. However, if you have super low energy, almost asleep, you would be on the other extreme on the Energy dimension at a 0, 1 or 2. Most likely, your Energy ratings will fall in the middle. Take a moment to note your Energy rating.

Move to Feelings. If, in this moment, you are feeling as pleasant and positive as you have ever felt, give yourself a 10 rating. How do you know how pleasant you feel? Pleasant feelings tend to be light and warm and if you are high in Pleasantness, that feeling might be reflected in your physical feelings as light and warmth. Then consider what the other extreme would feel like. A zero on the Feelings scale might feel cold, dark or perhaps heavy. Typically, your entries on Feelings will not be extreme but somewhere in the middle. Take a moment to note your Feelings rating. Now, take the two numbers (Energy and Feelings) and plot them on the *Mood Map*. Put a unique mark for the entry (such as numbers, letters or other symbols). You are not quite finished: look at the entry and ask yourself whether it accurately describes how you are feeling at this time. Adjust the entries as needed until it matches your ratings.

Plotting Other People's Feelings with the Mood Map

Asking someone their energy level and how pleasant they are feeling is a quick and easy way for determining someone's emotional state, though it may not be practical and seem a little odd in some contexts. We will provide some tips to help you get better at assessing someone's emotions later in the book.

It's very challenging to plot someone else on the Mood Map. It is probably even more complex and difficult to ask someone *else* to plot themselves on the Mood Map. Why is that? Consider how many times you've responded to the "how are you" question with a "great" even though you may have been a bit bored, tired, sad, annoyed, frustrated or anxious. All these feelings are probably not considered under the term "great." What if you just listen to *how* a person responds to your question? Again, this is very tricky because the moment someone asks us how we are doing, we may start to mask our true feelings and in a more energetic and pleasant tone than we feel, answer with an upbeat, "great." We also do not always want to share our true feelings with others. And, lastly, we may not really know how we feel.

Here are a few ways to get someone to accurately and honestly indicate where they are on the Mood Map:

1. Start with your current mood. Introduce the Mood Map and indicate your entry.

2. Then, turn to the other person and ask the below questions. Ask in a tone that invites openness and honesty and never push the person into revealing information they are uncomfortable sharing.

3. Where would you plot yourself on the Mood Map?

4. What caused you to feel this way? Anything else?

5. What word (or words) best describes how you feel?

6. If the answer seems dissonant or unclear, ask again about what caused the feeling.

7. How are you expressing this emotion?

8. Given where you are on the Mood Map, how will you reach the goals you set for yourself today?

If you hear a Mood Map response that is problematic – extreme sadness or anger for example, you can do two things—one, validate how they are feeling, "I can see how someone might feel that way.," and two, offer assistance, "Is there anything I can do to help?"

Be sure to thank the other person for sharing their current feelings! And, if a student provides a response that is troubling, make sure you utilize your school's counseling resources.

Mood Map, Primary Version

Younger students may struggle with labeling their feelings by assigning numbers to them. (Using negative numbers with the Mood Meter makes this process more difficult given we typically don't teach negative numbers until later in a student's career.) Therefore, you may find it easier to use a Mood Map without numbers, such as the one in Figure 3, and ask slightly different questions.

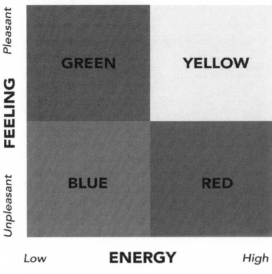

Figure 3: The Mood Map
(Primary Version)

Plotting Younger Students on the Primary Version of the Mood Map.
Here are a few ideas on how to ask younger children to plot themselves on the Mood Map.

Energy: Think about how much energy you have right now. If you are bursting full of energy you would score very high on the map. If you are really sleepy and moving slowly, you would score very low. Where do you think you are in terms of Energy?

Pleasantness: Now, how "pleasant" do you feel right now? Pleasant means how cheerful or how "good" you feel right now. Remember a time when you felt very pleasant – that feeling would chart very high on Pleasantness. Where do you think you are on Pleasantness?

Then help the child plot themselves on the unnumbered Mood Map. Follow the other instructions, for example, suggesting a word that describes that quadrant and checking in with the child to confirm it is accurate.

Helpful Questions to Map Emotions:

- Context – is the person acting differently than they normally do?
- Body language – what are their posture and movements telling me?
- Tone of voice – do their words match the tone of their voice?
- Silence – are they communicating effectively, or have they shut down?

Application

Here are some ideas on how to apply this skill.

A.   How to ask, "How are you?"

With practice, you will discover your own questions , but try to start with these:

- How you ask matters: Ask in a tone that invites a real, honest response.
- How has your day been so far?
- Tell me what's going on?
- What are your thoughts about ____?
- On a scale of 1 to 10 …. How do you feel about ___?
- How do you feel about this on a scale of 1 to 10 …? What would get you to a 10?
- What is on your mind?
- You seem ___. Is that right? (Low energy can be seen as low interest rather than being reflective.)

Culture is critical when mapping emotions. All cultures have what are called "display rules." Culture, in this context, refers to your school, your classroom, your family, your country of origin or the specific classroom you work in. Every place has its own display rules, and these rules determine which emotions can be shown and when and how they can be shown. In many situations, our felt emotions do not match our expressed emotions. Know your culture and ask a question that will generate an honest answer. Know when, when not and how to ask "how are you?."

B. Map Emotions Checklist

- ✓ Begin with you and ask, "How am I feeling?"
- ✓ Before beginning an important conversation, identify the emotional state of the other person/s.
- ✓ What is the emotional environment (vibe) in the room?
- ✓ How are people feeling during the discussion?
- ✓ Are you getting the results you desire?

C. Warnings and What to Watch For

- • Be hyper-aware of when you ask the "how are you" question and allow people to pass. You have a position of power over students and others, and you cannot, even unintentionally, abuse this power.
- • There are data on cross-cultural emotion perception inaccuracies. You must exercise even *greater* caution when mapping the emotions of diverse groups of people, especially those who differ from you in terms of various identities.

Interesting Fact: Each of us has a different "neutral" emotional facial expression. It's very difficult to know what your resting emotional expression looks like to others unless you can see it. Use a mirror or take selfies or, even better, use your webcam as you work, and video yourself over the course of routine tasks. Then play it back and see what you think and make adjustments accordingly.

MATCH EMOTIONS

Accurately mapping emotions, and knowing what emotions you and others are experiencing, is the critical beginning of emotional intelligence. The next step is determining whether these emotions will help you reach your intended goal. We call this "matching the mood to the task at hand."

Let's go back to the Mood Map and overlay it with the emotions for each of the four quadrants, and how these emotions can be useful depending on the situation. For example, you are about to go into a parent meeting to discuss a student who is facing discipline because of a physical fight with another student. Before the meeting you are feeling worried and a little overwhelmed. You know emotions are contagious and your current feelings won't be helpful to you or the parents. Remembering emotions direct your thinking and influence your behavior; you ask—"What emotions will help me and these parents have a productive discussion?"

Some people feel there are good and bad emotions, but in reality, all emotions serve a constructive purpose. Typically, anger is displayed when there is injustice, inequity or a dream not realized. Anger can and does drive positive growth and change. The passage of the *Education of All Handicapped Children's Act* in the United States in the 1970's required energy, determination and focus. If we simply accepted that some children were "warehoused," and meditated our way out of this sense of injustice, nothing would have changed!

Sadness is felt when there is loss, happiness when something is gained and fear when people feel threatened. We have spent a good deal of time and effort working through how to share the importance and helpful nature of all emotions. As we noted earlier, this is not a book about happiness or positive psychology, and to us, some of that work seems to focus purely on your own happiness and encourages you to filter out "negative" experiences and emotions. That's not helpful, and it's not what great educators should do. Life is difficult and filled with stressors and challenges. Emotions—anger, sadness, happiness—provide us with different perspectives on problems and all are necessary to engage with if you want to be an effective educator. The key is to match the emotion to the task. We know based on research that some emotions are more helpful than others, depending on the situation. Therefore, the next time you are about to go into a meeting or teach a lesson, determine what emotions are the most helpful to achieve your goal.

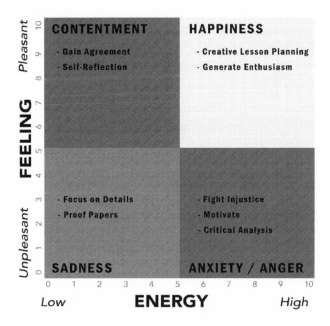

Figure 4: Map then Match

Emotional Lesson Planning

How, exactly, does matching emotions to the task, or goal, work? While Figure 4 is basic, it gives you enough of an idea on how to facilitate different tasks with different emotions. The phrase "match mood to task" can help you remember how emotions impact lesson plans and meetings. Consider this example. As an elementary school teacher you have some say over the flow of the day's lessons. You've already mapped how you and your students feel in the early afternoon, which is lower energy but mildly pleasant, in the Contentment quadrant of the Mood Map. Rather than fighting an uphill battle, what if you reviewed your day's lessons and inserted a reflective journaling lesson into the early afternoon slot? This simple change would leverage the emotions of the moment and enhance the learning that might not have happened otherwise. However, if the current emotions of the students aren't ideal, and you have to shift their emotions, we'll provide you with strategies to Move emotions from one quadrant to another later in the book. Table 2 provides you with a framework to Match emotions to the task, listing two examples and leaving room for you to enter your own emotionally-intelligent lesson planning. If the Matched to Task column is yes for both student and teacher, then there is no need to take action. However, if the emotions are not matched, you will have to Move emotions to a more ideal emotion.

Task	Day/Time	Students' Quadrant	Teacher's Quadrant	Ideal Quadrant	Matched to Task?
Edit essay	Tuesday 2nd period	Yellow	Red	Student: Blue Teacher: Green	Student: No Teacher: No
Reflective journaling	Friday 3rd period	Green	Yellow	Student: Green Teacher: Green	Student: Yes Teacher: No
Task:				Student: Teacher:	Student: Teacher:
Task:				Student: Teacher:	Student: Teacher:

Table 2: Match Mood to Task

Emotional Empathy and Connections

Not only are emotions important when performing tasks, they are also used to connect with people. Think of someone in your life who mentored you, gave you great advice or inspired you to be your best. Chances are they connected with you emotionally. We use emotions to show empathy, care and concern for others. Successful educators understand the importance of emotions to build meaningful relationships and understand how they can inspire and motivate others. More than that, great educators create an emotional climate that allows others to succeed. Sometimes that means lighting a fire under people to create a sense of urgency. Of course, there can be a downside to feeling what others feel. Emotional empathy, this feelings-based connection with others, can take a toll. If you feel what others feel, it can be draining. Psychologist Paul Bloom has a well-reasoned argument against emotional empathy[15], suggesting cognitive empathy (rational compassion) might be more effective. We have a different view. What if, rather than feeling less emotional empathy, we managed those feelings better? To us, that seems like a better solution than closing yourself off to the emotional world of others. While it is important to connect to others emotionally, you also need to ensure your own well-being. You will need to learn how to manage the impact others' emotions have on you, which we discuss later in the book when we get to the fourth ability of EI - Move emotions.

We want to caution you—while all emotions can be smart (including anger, anxiety and sadness)—we are not giving you license to act like a jerk. We explain more about expressing and moving emotions later, but you need to tread with great care around these strong, unpleasant emotions. Effectively moving emotions to effect change cannot be about enhancing your own status over that of others. You should generally not act in an angry manner, but you can allow anger

---

15   Bloom, P. (2016). *Against Empathy: The Case for Rational Compassion*. NY: Ecco.

to fuel change if, and only if, you have the emotion management expertise to harness its energy. Remember, over the long-term, great educators create a positive and supportive climate—the kind of environment where students and teachers bring their "A" game every day.

When fueling change, consider anger as raw energy, like a barrel of jet fuel. If you aren't careful and unwittingly toss a match into that barrel, it blows up in your face. Anger has a bad reputation, because people with lower EI try to harness the raw energy of anger and end up making things worse for themselves and others. However, people possessing finely-developed EI skills can take the same anger, the barrel of fuel, and harness it just as a high-performance jet engine takes jet fuel and uses it to power flight. (See Figure 5)

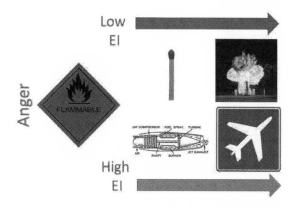

Figure 5: The Destructive and Constructive Power of Anger

Before you try to harness your anger to affect the greater good, ask yourself whether you are ready for the consequences. Be certain you possess the skills necessary to channel anger into a constructive process. Master the ability to effectively manage emotions. But, above all, make sure you are correct that anger is justified. That's where the ability to understand the Meaning of emotions comes into play, which we discuss later in the book.

Emotional Empathy and Emotional Labor

Educators engage in emotional labor every single day. While a strong emotional connection provides us with meaning and purpose, it can also be a source of burnout. We want to stress again the importance of developing your Move emotions skill before attempting to enhance your emotional empathy and emotional connections.

Helpful Questions for Matching Emotions:

- What emotions are we feeling?
- Are these emotions helpful to reach the goal? (Use Figure 4.)
- Am I using emotions to connect with others?
- Do I regularly engage with others' emotions?

Application

Here are some ideas on how to apply this skill.

A. Matching Mood to the Task at Hand

- What tasks do you do on a recurring basis? For example: lesson planning, grading, parent meetings.
- What emotions do you typically feel when you do these tasks?
- Are these emotions helpful to the task?
- What emotions would be *more* helpful?
- How can you generate a more helpful emotion before or during the task?

B. Matching Emotions Checklist

- ✓ Each day, look for opportunities to connect with others.
- ✓ Is there someone who needs your attention? Is someone displaying sadness, boredom, anger, frustration, etc.?
- ✓ Create a safe environment for a meaningful conversation that is confidential, non-judgmental, with no retribution.

✓ Practice deep listening—look for meaning in the words said and not said, body language (although this is extremely difficult to do well) and emotions.

✓ Seek to understand the other person's point of view—what's going on for them, what are they concerned about and how can you help?

C.   Warnings and What to Watch For

- Make sure you, your students or fellow teachers have the skill to move and manage emotions that are generated when developing your Match emotions skills. It is unfair to push emotions onto others, especially if they are not ready or prepared to experience those emotions.
- "I know how you feel" – we hear this often but we can never *truly* feel what others feel, we can only approximate their lived experience. Don't say to someone "I know how you feel." Instead, consider reflecting their feelings and physical sensations through your unambiguous non-verbal signals and some general, verbal statements. For example, an obvious smile combined with a clear "Wow! That sounds really exciting!" can send the message.
- The skills of EI need to be matched with cultural competence. Even the most empathetic person cannot begin to accurately "get" the emotional experience of another person if they lack this competence. Do not assume others' reactions to events are similar to yours. Do not assume you know how someone else feels. This skill, in the absence of cultural awareness and competence, can do great harm because you will assume a shared feeling when it does not exist.
- Develop your Move skills, discussed later in the book, before enhancing your emotional empathy.

Interesting Fact: Not convinced of the importance of emotions such as sadness and anger? You can read the research. Or, you can watch the Pixar animated movie "Inside Out"! Two emotions researchers consulted on the movie and the data behind it are very solid.

MEANING OF EMOTIONS

After accurately identifying emotions (Map), and determining which emotion would be more helpful to achieve the goal (Match), we need to understand why we feel the way we do and how emotions can shift and change over time (Meaning).

We are now seeking to understand what caused the emotion in the first place. You must understand the root cause of the emotion to know what it means—whether it represents actionable data or not. Educators frequently make the mistake of hypothesizing the reason behind others' emotions, or avoid them entirely, because knowing the reason can be uncomfortable. Instead of avoiding emotions, get curious. Take time to think about the person—what emotions are they experiencing, what might be the cause for their emotion and how can you help move them to a better place?

Take a moment to think of the people you rely on for your success. Perhaps it's your principal, your fellow teachers, other colleagues or your students. Now ask yourself—what makes each person "tick"? That is, do you know what makes them happy, sad, bored, excited, frustrated, proud, disgusted and angry? To communicate and collaborate effectively with others, you need to know them really well. And you need to meet them where they are; instead of following the golden rule of treating them as *you* would want to be treated, follow the platinum rule—treat them as *they* want to be treated.

Getting to know what makes people tick takes time and practice. Some people will make it easy for you and are happy to share their emotions, interests and passions. However, others will not, depending on their personality, culture, life experiences and comfort level with sharing this type of information—especially with their teacher or administrator. However, by demonstrating your understanding of others, you can more readily connect with them to move them towards where they need to be to reach goals and objectives.

Understand What Makes Educators Tick

As mentioned earlier, some people will tell you exactly how they're feeling and why they feel the way they do. Others will challenge you to figure out what's going on with them. To begin understanding others, they need to trust your intentions. Let them know why you want to get to know them better. Share with them how you want to be a better teacher, administrator or colleague and to do this, you want to know what is important to them. You don't have to get personal, you can start with work (see Table 3).

Asking questions such as, "What do you like most about your work? What frustrates you at school? What makes you bored? What really fires you up? What do you look forward to? How do you like to spend your time? What do you look forward to on school breaks?" Once you begin this conversation, you may be surprised where it leads. Next, be attentive when they express emotion—what emotion did you see? What was the cause? Over time, you begin to understand what makes the person tick without even asking. While understanding others' emotions is a critical part of EI, always remember to respect others' privacy.

Emotion	General Cause	Application	Example
Frustration	What aspect of the work frustrates you?	Minimize annoying tasks	*Provide a safe environment to share concerns*
Boredom	What tasks do you find dull?	Assign and reassign tasks	*Empower teachers to find new ways for doing mundane work*
Happiness	What type of work do you enjoy?	Align work to person's strengths	*Find opportunities to showcase strengths more*

Emotion	General Cause	Application	Example
Pride	What accomplishments at work are you most proud of?	Understand how to motivate	*Tailor recognition to the person—formal, informal, or a simple thank you*

Table 3. Understanding Emotions for Educators

Of course, these questions won't work and are not appropriate with students. However, the same idea applies to students, just with different questions. Here, too, the students' ages matter and we present a few ways to ask these questions in Table 4.

Emotion	General Cause	Application	Example
Frustration	What aspects of school frustrate you?	Increase student engagement and attentiveness	*Is there something about school you do not like?* *What parts of the day annoy you?*
Boredom	What tasks do you find dull?	Assign and reassign tasks	*Empower students to find new ways for doing mundane work*
Happiness	What type of work do you enjoy?	Align work to person's strengths	*What is the best part of your school day?* *What do you most enjoy at school?*
Pride	What accomplishments at work are you most proud of?	Understand how to motivate	*What have you done at school you are proud of?* *What is your best subject or part of school?*

Table 4. Understanding Emotions for Students

Use Your Words!

To be an emotionally intelligent educator, use words carefully. Don't just toss out any emotion word to express how you feel; select the best emotion word to convey meaning, get people's attention and help them understand the situation. Don't say you are enraged if you are merely annoyed—that only confuses people. If you go to red alert all the time, your colleagues will avoid you and you may lose credibility. Conversely, if you have been promised an overdue homework assignment for days, and your student fails to deliver, you can legitimately say you are disappointed and perhaps annoyed. The key is to accurately describe the emotions you are feeling so others understand what you are experiencing and why. Table 5 adds helpful emotion words for you to use to better communicate exactly how you are feeling.

Emotion	General Cause	Words
Frustration	Blocked from getting something you want and value.	*Irritated* *Annoyed* *Frustrated* *Angry* *Enraged*
Disgust	Your values are violated or offended.	*Distasteful* *Objectionable* *Disgusted* *Loathsome*
Happiness	Gain something you value.	*Contented* *Pleased* *Happy* *Delighted* *Joyous*

Emotion	General Cause	Words
Worry	Possible threat.	*Concerned* *Worried* *Anxious* *Afraid* *Terror*
Surprise	Something unexpected.	*Distracted* *Interested* *Surprised* *Amazed* *Shocked*
Sadness	Lose something you value.	*Pensive* *Disappointed* *Sad* *Miserable* *Depressed*

Table 5. Emotion Words at Work

To better understand emotions, it helps to build your emotion vocabulary and understand how emotions progress and blend to form more complex emotions. One simple way to do this is by studying the simple illustration of emotions (Figure 6).

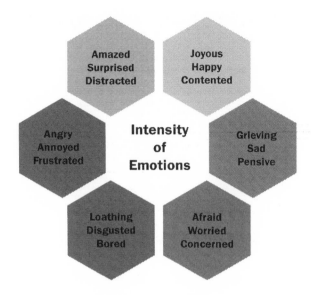

Figure 6: Emotion Wheel

If you are interested in a beautiful mathematical representation of emotions, search for "Plutchik Emotion Circumplex" on the Web, to see an interesting illustration of how emotions progress. Emotions can progress from less to more intense if whatever caused the initial emotion continues to occur. For example, annoyance, when left unattended, can lead to anger, which can then lead to rage. Boredom can lead to disgust, which can lead to loathing if unattended. Therefore, it is critical to identify the initial emotion early, especially unpleasant emotions, so the situation doesn't escalate into something that could have an unintended impact on your classroom or school.

Not only do emotions progress, they also blend to form more complex emotions. The emotions of joy and trust blend and become love, and disgust and anger blend and become contempt. Emotions have many nuances and are often mislabeled. Often, people say they are angry when in reality they are frustrated, which is a milder emotion. Or, they say they *love* school, when they are really only interested (mild). The more accurate we are at naming emotions, the better we can uncover the cause of the emotion and move it in a more helpful direction.

Feelings, Moods, Emotions: *Feelings are not always facts – but emotions are data*

Understanding emotions can be confusing when we use the words feelings, moods and emotions interchangeably—even in this book. To get better at understanding feelings remember this: a mood is something that is general, diffuse and often unclear. For example, we often say we woke up on the "wrong side of the bed," or we are in a "foul" mood. We try to understand why we feel the way we do, but we just can't, or we realize we are feeling "off" or "cranky." Therefore, it's important to move the mood (which we'll discuss in the next section of the book). However, if upon examining how we feel there is a source, this is data we can use to make better decisions. In short, you should attend to the feeling you have, but analyze its source. If it's a mood, Move it; if it's an emotion, Match it. Figure 7 depicts how a "feelings decision tree" might look.

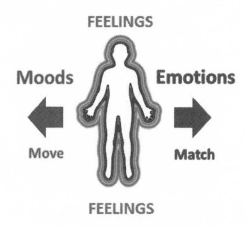

Figure 7: Feelings Are Not Always Facts

Let's apply this to the classroom. In this example, you have a student with an "attitude" and when he disrupted class this morning, your gut told you to take action, otherwise things could escalate. As a result of your action, things quickly got out of control which resulted in sending him to the assistant principal's office. Because you were motivated to act on your feelings, without thinking about them first, you and your student now have to deal with an unintended consequence you both did not want. This is what happens when we demonstrate low emotional intelligence and do not understand the Meaning of emotions. Often, we are told to trust our gut, go with our instinct or listen to our feelings. Listening to feelings is one thing, and we agree with that advice, but we strongly advise you <u>not</u> to trust your gut instinct or feelings until you analyze them and their source. It is critical for everyone, but especially educators who must form emotional bonds with students, to reflect on the causes of their feelings and consider the reasonableness of their feelings and reactions to events. In this example, your baseline mood that morning was on the unpleasant side. Perhaps you went to sleep much too late, slept through your alarm, missed breakfast, had a disagreement with your partner, the commute was extra difficult and you got to school too late to grab your morning coffee. Any one of these occurrences can leave you not exactly feeling at your best. Unfortunately, if you begin your day feeling unpleasant (or as most of us say, in a "bad" mood), it won't take much to set you off or take long before small hassles become giant ones. An emotionally intelligent leader knows its best to get to the root cause of the emotion before taking action.

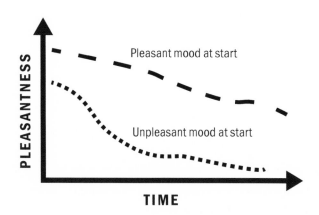

Figure 8. Impact of background mood on your reaction over time

Figure 8 illustrates how people starting off in a bad mood can spiral into more unpleasant emotions over time compared to people who start in a more pleasant mood when reacting to the <u>same</u> events. The lesson being—before acting on your feelings, analyze their many sources. Ask yourself these questions:

- What is my starting level of pleasantness?
- How much of my reaction is due to my overall mood?
- How much of my reaction is due to what happened?
- Would someone else feel the same way I do?
- Is it possible I am just in a bad mood?

The answers to these questions will help you better analyze the sources of your feelings and determine whether you are overreacting or if it represents a signal that something happened that requires your attention and action. Use the feelings decision tree in Figure 9 to decide.

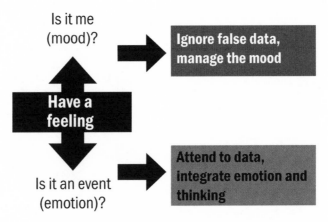

Figure 9. Don't Always Trust Your Gut!

Being able to discern between a mood and an emotion requires utmost skill. With a little bit of guided reflection and using Table 6 as a guide, you can discover and uncover the source of your feelings. The key take-away to remember is: emotions are data but feelings are not always facts!

Summary	
Describe the event:	
My initial Pleasantness level:	0.....1.....2.....3.....4.....5.....6.....7.....8.....9.....10
My Pleasantness level during event:	0.....1.....2.....3.....4.....5.....6.....7.....8.....9.....10
Reflect on possible causes:	
What else is happening around this time that *might* impact my mood?	[ ] Physiological (e.g., sleep, illness) [ ] Unrelated events (e.g., argument, interactions)
Is it *possible* I was just in a bad mood?	[ ] Yes [ ] Maybe [ ] No
Would I have reacted the same way on a different day?	[ ] Yes [ ] Maybe [ ] No
How would another person react to this situation?	[ ] Similar Way [ ] Differently
Indicate a percentage for each question below (they should add up to 100%):	
Cause of my feeling(s) due to my starting mood	0...10...20...30...40...50...60...70...80...90...100
Cause of my feeling(s) due to the event	0...10...20...30...40...50...60...70...80...90...100
Decision: it is a mood or is it an emotion?	
How should I interpret and react to this event?	[ ] Do not react: use Move strategies to change the mood [ ] Reduce my reaction: use Move strategies [ ] Something happened, it wasn't just me, attend to event and the data of my feelings

Table 6. Is It a Feeling or a Fact?

Helpful Questions and Tips for Making Meaning of Emotions:

- Develop and enhance your emotion vocabulary to better communicate ideas.
- Whom do I rely on for my success?
- Do I know what makes this person – student, teacher, parent—tick?
- Do I understand why they feel the way they do?
- Do I know how to move them to a place they need to be to reach their goal?
- Do I understand why I feel the way I do? Is it a mood (Move it) or is it an emotion (data) I should be paying attention to (Match it)?
- Do I share with people what makes me tick so they can communicate with me more effectively?
- Remember—feelings are not always facts; moods can be wrong, but emotions are data.

Application

Here are some ideas on how to apply this skill.

A. Emotional What-If?

- Before your next lesson or meeting conduct an emotional "what-if" analysis of what could possibly happen?
- What is the goal of the meeting?
- What is the best time and place for this meeting to ensure we are at our best?
- Knowing the other person as well as I do, how might the person react to what I need to tell them?
- What questions will I ask, what tone of voice should I use, what is the best body language?
- If they react negatively, what can I do to keep the conversation going in a positive direction? If they react positively, how do I acknowledge or capitalize on that for the goals set out?

- Can I show more empathy, listen more, seek a common goal? How can I use precise emotion terms to demonstrate this?

B. Meaning of Emotions Checklist

- ✓ Consider the source of your feelings
- ✓ Do not act on a feeling until you truly understand its source
- ✓ Review the day and your feelings to consider how much of the feeling is due to a mood and how much to an emotion
- ✓ Ask yourself whether someone else would feel the same way and whether the feeling is reasonable
- ✓ If the feeling is mostly a mood—ignore and move it (Move)
- ✓ If the feeling is mostly an emotion—attend to it and act on it (Match)

C. Warnings and What to Watch For

- Do not ask someone for their emotion causes unless you will, 1) remember what the person tells you, and 2) employ this knowledge to strengthen the relationship. In other words, if you signal you care about someone and do not follow through, it can be hurtful.
- When you do forget an individual's unique emotion cause, note it and apologize.
- You need to apply this skill through the lens of cultural competence, or as CASEL suggests, "examine the various social and cultural identities of oneself and others, understand and appreciate diversity from a historically grounded and strengths-focused lens." If you fail to take the perspective of others, you will appear to lack cognitive empathy, you will not be able to "get" someone else and worse, you will think you have.
- As always, watch the power dynamic of a teacher asking a student, or an administrator asking a teacher for their emotion causes. Mutual sharing is one way to reduce the possible misuse of this strategy, but please be careful and vigilant to not abuse the technique.

41

Interesting Fact: Teachers often understand the importance of getting to know their students but few share with them what makes them "tick." If you don't share what makes you happy, proud, frustrated or angry with others, then you could be setting yourself up for disappointment. How will your students know what to do more, or less of, if you don't tell them? You don't have to reveal personal details of your life, you could say something like "It is frustrating to me when you say you will hand in your homework the next day and then you forget."

MOVE EMOTIONS

The last step in the EI framework is Moving emotions. It is the easiest ability to grasp, and the most difficult to execute. The prior three abilities of Map, Match and Meaning can be performed perfectly, but moving your emotion, and those of others, will determine if you behave in an emotionally intelligent manner. You are constantly being assessed by your interactions with others, so it's critical to get proficient at both moving your emotions, and the emotions of those around you.

The first step in moving your emotions, especially unpleasant ones, is to be aware of how emotions show up in your body. Many people feel anger in their chest, throat or jaw. Some feel fear when they get goosebumps or the hair rises on the back of their neck. Joy is frequently experienced with a lightness in the body and warmth in the heart. For each person it is different. Ask yourself, where do certain emotions typically show up in my body? By being aware, you can react appropriately when your body sends you a signal. This ability is critical and takes practice, and lots of it. Unfortunately, unanalyzed feelings can lead us to make terrible decisions or say things we regret. However, listening to our body allows our brain to catch up with the emotion, to fully process why we feel the way we do and reminds us of the goal we want to achieve so we can make the best decision, regardless of what emotions we feel.

In school, we are often told to suppress our emotions, and as educators we keep tamping them down. It's fine to suppress emotional displays from time to time. The show must go on, the lesson must be taught, and we cannot always and should not always be constantly emoting. At the same time, constantly holding everything in, despite how we feel, is neither sustainable nor recommended. If you suppress emotions too long, they may come out in inappropriate ways and have unintended consequences. Eventually, suppressed anger may lead to destructive rage and devastating results. Conversely, bottling up emotions may make you appear fake, inauthentic or uncaring. Bottom line, the constant and frequent suppression of emotion is unhealthy for everyone and eventually erodes trust and relationships.

The best strategies for moving emotions are the long-term ones: adequate sleep, healthy food, exercise, social support, spiritual practices, prayer, meditation and relaxation. We know long-term strategies are what we *should* be doing, but we often don't do what's best for us! There are other short-term strategies you can use as well. Depending on the situation, you may choose either strategic or responsive approaches—or both. Think of a time when you were in a meeting and someone or something got you really annoyed. Chances are you felt it—perhaps a tightness in your chest or you felt hot in the face. Everyone looks at you to see how you will respond. This is where the rubber hits the road—what strategy are you going to use to reach the goal you set for the meeting? How will you say it? What tone of voice? How will you keep the meeting on track?

Moving emotions doesn't only include *you*. By behaving in an emotionally intelligent manner you will also be able to move other people's emotions. This concept may seem odd because you're probably thinking you can't control other people's emotions, which is true. However, your response to other's emotions can greatly impact the effectiveness of the conversation. For example, let's say you are giving a teacher critical feedback and they become angry or perhaps they become sad and begin to cry. There are many strategies you can use to continue the dialogue—showing empathy, listening, seeking understanding, being supportive, showing care and working towards a common goal.

The key to helping others move their emotions is to lead by example and move your own emotions during the conversation. How can you remain neutral, or at times generate a positive state? It's okay, and can be very intelligent to be angry, but it is rarely a good idea to act aggressively. How can you establish an environment for others to share what is important to them? How can you show empathy while still reaching your shared goal? How can you light a fire under an unmotivated teacher. Moving emotions successfully takes practice, but if you stay open to all types of emotion, you will connect and communicate with others more effectively. Refer to Table 7 when you need effective, and easy, strategies for moving *your* emotions.

Strategy	Example
Prepare	Do a quick run-through of possible outcomes, not just desired or expected outcomes. For example, ask yourself, "Is it *possible* my new teacher will become defensive when I give him his year-end evaluation?"
Modify Mood	If you know your current emotion isn't helpful to your goal—change it! Psych yourself up before a big meeting or calm yourself down if you need to get your "game face" on.
Reappraise	We all act badly at times, but few of us are real jerks. We may act out because we have something going on in our lives. Consider whether the other person—student, parent, teacher, administrator—is just having a bad day. Ask yourself, "How does the other person view the situation?" or "Is it possible I am wrong about their intentions?"
Self-talk	Use your inner voice and repeat some calming or motivational thoughts to get through stressful moments. For example, "I can do this. It's all good, I'm okay. This too shall pass."
Physiological	Take a deep breath, just one to start. Stand up or stretch. Or simply smile—the facial feedback hypothesis suggests that merely smiling will elevate your mood. None of these take a lot of time and the benefits are long lasting.
Intervening Moment	Take a moment to pause, count to three, take one deep breath. If you have more time, write down what you'd like to say, but don't. Take a short break. Draft a response of what you'd like to say, but do not send until you can edit, when you have a more pleasant disposition.
Express a Different Emotion	If you cannot change the time of a meeting or the situation, and the show must go on, express the *desired* emotion. It's not suppressing, it is expressing and generating a more helpful emotion.

Strategy	Example
Long Term	You know these techniques—your goal should be to select one and give it a try, something you are most likely to implement. Techniques include: get adequate sleep, eat a healthy diet, pray, meditate, have fun, seek social support, get some exercise. Monitor your consumption of social media and make different choices of what you read and view.
Relationships	Although this is also a long-term strategy it's important enough to list on its own. Cherish your family, friends and cultivate good colleagues. And be a good friend and colleague to others. Strong social networks are vital to our long-term emotional health.

Table 7. Emotion Management Strategies—You

Once you master effective emotion management strategies for yourself, you will begin to notice an improvement in your ability to move other people's emotions. Moving emotions is not manipulative; if you connect with other people and feel for them, you will "do the right thing." In Table 8, is a list of emotion management strategies to use with other people. You will invariably make mistakes when practicing this ability, so be ready with one of the best emotion management strategies in the world—a heartfelt apology.

Strategy	Example
Distraction	If the situation is on an extreme downward spiral, or if the time or place is not appropriate for a difficult conversation, the idea is to quickly change the subject. You might say "Hey, let's grab a cup of coffee," with a peer, or "Let's come back to this problem later," with a student. Use this strategy sparingly, otherwise you will never successfully address the underlying issues.
Select or Modify Situation	Modify the situation to increase the odds of achieving your goal, such as when and where you meet. And you can verbalize the reason if you wish: "Monday's are really hectic, so let's have our weekly review meeting on Tuesday mornings." Even consider where you sit in a meeting (behind a desk, next to the person, standing up, in a hallway and so forth). Consider the time of day and day of the week to have a discussion. In short—have the conversation when you're at your best!
Change Situation	Take a break and indicate the need to change the tone. Try this, for example: "I need to think about this for a few minutes. Let's come back in 5 minutes and when we do, I'd like to move on to the second topic." When meetings get off track you can say "Let's take a few minutes and when we return, refocus on the goal for our meeting." Other strategies include moving your chair or asking the person to come to a different room with you.
Emotional Connection	No one knows what you are thinking, so demonstrate you care by saying something like, "That sounds difficult. I am really sorry. What can I do to support you? What do you need right now?"
Match and Validate	A specific emotional connection strategy is to acknowledge the other person. Saying, "You shouldn't feel that way," invalidates the other person's views and feelings. Whether you agree or not, it is not up to you to argue how the person should feel. None of us knows what the other person is experiencing. Instead of arguing, try this powerful phrase, "I can see how someone might feel that way."[16]

---

16   This is from dialectical behavior therapy.

Strategy	Example
Modulate Tone	Change your tone and get people's attention. Increase or decrease the volume and pitch of your speech to either calm things down or energize the other person.
Physiological Techniques	Have walking meetings, lunch meetings, take breaks. Stand up every now and then. Many schools encourage students to take breaks within the classroom. Just make sure your classroom has a way to track how often and how long students break for and build scaffolds so eventually they use these techniques to help self-regulate without losing instructional time.
Express Concern	Similar to Emotional Connection, simply tell the other, "I am sorry to hear that" and perhaps follow-up with, " How can I help? What would you like me to do? What can I do?"
Intervening Moment	Before taking action, take a moment to pause. You can simply look down for a moment and consciously breathe. Buy some time—there is often no need to commit yourself to a position or an answer. Tell the other person "Let me think about this" or "I will get back to you."

Table 8. Emotion Management Strategies—Others

It's Not All About Being Positive and Relaxed

Recall the lessons and tips from Matching emotions, that all emotions can be smart. The goal of emotion management is not to relax and engage in positive emotions all of the time. The goal of moving emotions is not a single-minded focus on your well-being. Some people suggest doing things like disengaging from reading the latest news in order to maintain peaceful tranquility. We recognize life is filled with stress, and there are times when you need to turn off and disconnect (we do support turning your phone off, for example!). But at the same time, many people do not have the luxury or privilege of not thinking about the latest headlines because they live these headlines every day.

Our goal is not to have you be a happy, upbeat, cheery, positive person all the time. We want you to engage, and grapple with, the tough challenges facing educators, and to succeed at those challenges. We want you, in short, to change the world and make it a better place to live. At the same time, we urge you to fill up your emotional reserves. It is important to recognize when you're feeling overwhelmed and to practice self-care. The goal of emotional intelligence is not to keep a smile on your face and be constantly happy—it is to give you the skills, focus and energy so you have the emotional resources to engage with the world's problems. You need to be at your best if you are engaging in the struggle to create change and drive innovation in your school or classroom. Another benefit of successfully deploying these emotion management strategies? You won't always bring your work problems home and therefore, be more emotionally available to your family and friends.

Helpful Questions and Tips for Moving Emotions:

Just like keeping a vehicle or bicycle going in the same direction requires constant, small course corrections, you must constantly move your emotions to maintain a steady state!

- Am I getting enough sleep, exercise, healthy food, relaxation, social support?
- Do I recognize where emotions show up in my body?
- Before reacting, do I take time to think about my response? What is my goal? How do I keep things moving in a positive direction?
- Do I stay open to other people's feelings? Do I show empathy? Do I try to understand their point of view? Do I listen? Do I support them while still holding them accountable?
- Do I show my emotions genuinely?
- Do I use my emotions to inspire, motivate, communicate and connect to others?

Application

Here are some ideas on how to apply these skills.

A. Filling Up Your Emotional Reserve:

To give your best, you must be your best, which means taking care of yourself so you have the energy to tackle challenges head-on.

- Take a moment to think of the activities you do when you feel completely fulfilled, happy, peaceful, re-energized or relaxed.
- Write down these activities until you can't think of anything else to add.
- Review the list and circle three activities you will commit to doing in the next week.
- Try to do at least three activities a week from your list for at least a month. Better yet—find someone who will help you stay committed to these activities or will do some of them with you!

B. Moving Others' Emotions Checklist

- ✓ Have you created a safe environment for others?
- ✓ What are the emotions you are seeing and sensing?
- ✓ Are these emotions helpful in the situation?
- ✓ Is your emotional state helpful?
- ✓ If not, what emotional management strategies will you use?

C. Move Anxiety and Anger Checklist

- ✓ If anger or anxiety are the ideal emotions for the task, you can only leverage them if you have extraordinary emotion management skills.
- ✓ Check to make sure the anger is justified—make sure it's not just a mood and make sure it's not personal.
- ✓ Use any and all of the self-management strategies.

✓ Reconsider the underlying causes of your anger in a calmer state; would someone else feel the same way for example?

✓ Practice a scenario in your head where you explain the frustration to others and consider multiple "what-if" analyses to determine the best way to convey the message.

✓ Ask yourself—is it worth it? Will showing unpleasant emotions damage the relationship I've tried so hard to establish?

✓ The message will only get through if people do not feel attacked.

✓ Now, in a calm and focused state, where you can accurately Map, Match and understand the Meaning of emotions, express your frustration using emotion vocabulary.

D.   Warnings and What to Watch For

- Teachers experience high levels of burnout and stress, thus the need for these self-focused emotion management strategies. We want you to stay engaged, to shine and to thrive!

- However, many teachers and educators experience dissatisfaction with their careers due to external factors such as frequent high-stakes testing, mandated curricula, crowded classrooms, underfunded schools and so forth. These factors can be demoralizing, which differs from burnout. Demoralization requires systemic change, it is not something you can meditate your way out of.

- Even those with high levels of emotional intelligence will not be able to successfully Move emotions all the time. Expect setbacks – practice these skills, seek feedback, tweak your approach and try again.

- Remember it is okay to suppress emotions at times! In fact, sometimes silence is golden and is the best and most appropriate strategy.

- Teachers: do not practice on your students! Administrators: do not practice emotional intelligence on your teachers! You have to apply these techniques and skills with care and at a high level of proficiency. Start with peers, get feedback, refine your approach and then deploy these strategies more broadly.

- Once again, we remind you of the importance of embedding these skills in a framework of cultural competence. CASEL notes the need for educators to "recognize and respond to cultural demands and opportunities and build relationships across cultural backgrounds."

Interesting Fact: Many teachers feel they are experts at suppressing emotion and think they have a "poker face." Unfortunately, that isn't always the case. Emotions—especially anger, frustration and surprise—are difficult to disguise well. And even if you are good at it, if you didn't show emotion in certain situations, your students or others might feel that the issue isn't important or worse you don't care what happens.

SUMMARY

As you can see, dealing with emotions can be challenging, but it doesn't have to be impossibly difficult now that you have an understanding of how the four hard skills of emotional intelligence work together. This knowledge, along with a lot of practice and constructive feedback, will help you establish trusting relationships and hopefully lead to greater success for you, your students and your school. Part Two of this book provides you with concrete examples of challenges you will undoubtedly face as an educator, along with suggestions on how to apply the four EI skills using the Emotional Intelligence Blueprint.

Emotions in educational settings, when used effectively, can propel classrooms, schools, teachers, students and administrators to greatness. When used ineffectively, emotions can lead to recrimination, blame, stress and failure. Emotions are important. Emotions are what build relationships and trust. Emotions help us learn. Emotions connect people and are the fabric of what makes life meaningful. Emotions can be channeled to inspire, motivate and innovate. Will you be an emotionally intelligent educator, or allow emotions to lead you? Are you ready to model emotional intelligence, share with others what you have learned and embed it in how you teach and lead so it becomes part of your school culture? Interacting with happy students, teachers, parents or staff is easy; dealing with people who are experiencing anger or sadness takes great care, a lot of emotional intelligence knowledge and finely-honed skills. Forming relationships and establishing trust in the classroom is the bedrock of teaching. The choice you have is how you interact with emotions. Whether you perceive them or not, emotions exist, emotions matter and they impact every aspect of educational leadership.

Ask yourself:

- Can I accurately Map emotions in myself and others?
- Do I Match emotions to accomplish the task at hand and connect with others?
- Do I understand the Meaning of the emotions of others and what motivates, inspires, worries and frustrates them?
- Do I effectively Move my emotions and those of others to reach shared goals?

If you answered yes to these questions, ask an additional question—How do you know? Consider whether it is possible you are wrong, and then check your perceptions with others. If the answers are still yes, terrific, you have a powerful tool to use in your personal and professional life. If you answered sometimes, don't worry, with practice, combined with corrective feedback, you will improve. It does take time, but if you really care about it, you'll keep practicing and asking for feedback. Practice alone does not make you a more emotionally intelligent educator, you must get feedback! And if the answer is no, do not despair. That you read this book is a wonderful first step. Just as approaches to SEL should be strengths-based, so is this approach to EI. You possess emotional intelligence skills, of that we have no doubt. These skills emerge as we develop and grow as a person. We all can improve these skills. As we noted earlier, recent research, especially meta-analyses (a study of multiple studies), indicate EI can be learned and increased, and this includes studies of the ability model of EI. You can also learn compensatory or remedial strategies. Whether you have a background in special education or not, consider the purpose of an Individual Educational Plan (IEP) for a student with a non-verbal learning challenge. This student may struggle with reading comprehension, skipping lines on a page. Recall we earlier spoke about a "GPS" for emotions. While you may not "fix" that particular non-verbal learning challenge, you can change the outcome by simply using a program to display one line at a time, or even resorting to the old ruler trick: moving a ruler down a printed page, line by line. And without much effort, the student's reading comprehension soars. Think of the ideas in this book as your IEP for emotions that provides you with strategies for improving your EI performance as an educator.

Even for those who are skilled in EI, getting this right is not easy. To further your EI development, there are coaches who specialize in EI and can help you hone your EI skills. We've also included in the last section of the book, additional information, research and resources for you to continue your EI journey. We hope you continue developing EI and share your knowledge with students, colleagues and administrators.

PART TWO

The Educator's Practical Guide to Emotional Intelligence Blueprints

Developing and leveraging the four EI skills can be very helpful and ideally you will employ them real-time, following a multi-step process we call an Emotional Intelligence "Blueprint." We first employed this structured approach to solving difficult challenges about 20 years ago when an organization of analytical professionals asked for EI training. What better way to explain the importance of emotions than to use their language, and so, we presented them with the "Blueprint"[17]. Since that time, we've used the Blueprint in many different situations and have taught it to both teachers and students of all ages. It's a very simple process. The key is to use the approach to create environments where students, teachers, parents and educators all succeed, that is, to use it on a *prospective* basis. We'll provide you with Blueprints of common, difficult challenges educators face each and every day. In the next section you'll find a helpful template for you to create your own Blueprints.

Putting It All Together (The EI Blueprint)

You've begun leveraging the four abilities of emotional intelligence and now comes one of the more rewarding and valuable aspects of the ability model—putting it all together to be a more emotionally intelligent educator. In summary, everything you learned in

---

17   The Blueprint also appeared in the 2004 book, *The Emotionally Intelligent Manager* (Caruso & Salovey).

this book works together seamlessly as outlined in the EI Blueprint (Figure 10).

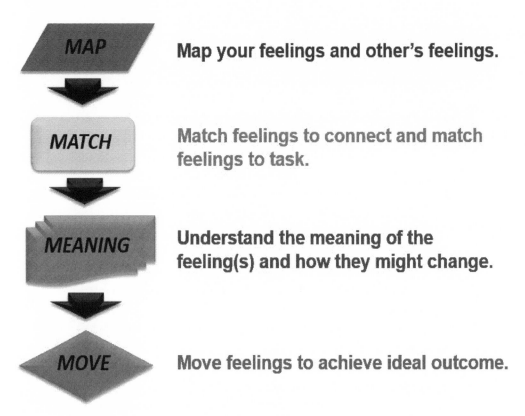

Map your feelings and other's feelings.

Match feelings to connect and match feelings to task.

Understand the meaning of the feeling(s) and how they might change.

Move feelings to achieve ideal outcome.

Figure 10. EI Blueprint

The Emotional Intelligence Blueprint Approach

The Blueprint approach can help you determine underlying, or root causes of difficult challenges you face as an educator. You can also use it as a journal, walk through it with someone if you're struggling with objectivity or being completely candid about the situation. You can even complete it to deconstruct an emotional encounter that didn't go as well as you hoped. We consider the Blueprint a "container" that steps you through the four emotional intelligence abilities to see different ways to Move emotions. There will be times when you get it partially or completely wrong. As we said, behaving in an emotionally intelligent manner, even for the most skilled, takes deliberate effort and practice with feedback.

We provide you with a number of Blueprints to help you solve your most critical challenges to create environments of respect and enhance learning in your schools. Our Blueprints will not exactly mirror your situation, and this is where your analytical ability comes into play. Analyze your situation, seek out the most similar Blueprint, and then adapt it to your specific situation. Even better, use the generic Blueprint process to create and then evaluate your own circumstance. As you engage in the behaviors suggested by a specific Blueprint, determine how you are feeling (Map) and whether those feelings are helpful or not (Match). Determine how the situation might unfold (Meaning) and manage (Move) your emotions and those of others in real-time to achieve your goal.

In the following Blueprints, we indicate the EI skill of the person relating the story, whether lower, average or higher. Some of the Blueprints are situations that went well, and others describe situations where a more considered use of emotional intelligence skills might have resulted in a more productive outcome. You will not always achieve successful results, even when the approach is used with the highest level of skill, but you will always be able to grow and develop as an educator and generate better outcomes.

Our Blueprints were created using input from educators on the front line who shared their day to day challenges with us. To protect their identities, we changed information such as names, grades and gender identity. We've created a set of Blueprints focusing on teachers and another set of Blueprints focusing on leadership and administration. We'd love to hear from <u>you</u> with stories of your own challenges and how you addressed them using an *EI Blueprint*[18].

---

18   Email us at blueprint@eiteacher.com.

TEACHER BLUEPRINTS

We start with the complex environment of classroom teachers and present a series of EI Blueprints addressing challenges they often face. The first few Blueprints address intrapersonal challenges teachers face and we then provide you with Blueprints focused on teacher-student or classroom management situations.

WAIT TIME WORRIES[19]

EI LEVEL This teacher has a **higher** level of EI skill

LOWER	AVERAGE	HIGHER

BACKGROUND Patience is not really my strength. That's why I wanted to be a high school teacher instead of teaching primary school. I've always liked things to happen fast! When I received feedback from my principal that I needed to improve my wait time (the amount of time I provide students to answer a question), I was not entirely surprised. Like all the feedback I receive, I went right to work on improving my instructional technique. To say I struggled is an understatement. I'd ask a question and make it about one second of wait time before I moved on to another student. There's just something about the flow of the discourse getting bogged down that made it difficult for me to pause and have moments of silence. Since I've taken some courses around EI before, I decided to blueprint my reaction so I can be more successful in this area next time.

GOAL Improve my wait time to increase my effectiveness and engage my students.

MAP *What are the emotions of you and others?* I feel *anxious* when there's dead space in the classroom. I feel like the flow of the lesson gets disrupted and nothing's happening. If there is no sound or writing I feel like I am wasting everyone's time and not doing my job. As I was blueprinting, I realized students in my classroom probably feel really rushed if they don't have the answer on the tip of their tongue.

---

19   Every Blueprint disguises the identity of the educator, student and school.

My quick pace probably creates *anxiety* in my students and perhaps they perceive me as *disinterested* in what they have to say. This makes it less likely for me to be able to get a range of viewpoints and checks for understanding in my class. I have to make this more about my students and less about my feelings.

MATCH *What emotions are most helpful?* I need to reduce my feelings of anxiety and increase my feelings of patience. I want students to feel like they have time to think through the questions when they answer. I should be able to get to 3-5 seconds of wait time if I can catch my own *irritation* and give my kids time to think. As I think back on the quadrants of the Mood Map, it seems green, being reflective, would be extremely helpful to both me and my students. This is a pleasant, but lower energy tone rather than my intense, burst of energy style when I get engaged with the material. My energy may be too much and too soon for my students and I end up pushing them away and not connecting.

MEANING *What is the cause of these emotions?* I hadn't realized this before, but there's a certain feeling of frustration I have when kids are struggling with an idea or a concept. I know I should be patient and caring, and I want to, but when I actually think about it, it's a frustrating experience! In fact, I went back through videos of me teaching and I realized I interacted more with the kids who had an easier time grasping the concepts in the lesson because they made me feel more successful as a teacher. Now I realize wait time is just the tip of the iceberg; my feelings impact a great deal of my teaching strategies. I also wonder whether my pace sends an unintended message to my students that I don't really care what they have to say. I do, but I realize it is possible they experience a different reality. First things first though, I'm going to improve my wait time so more students can feel confident to participate.

MOVE *How will you sustain or move these emotions?* Mapping my emotions, taking a running pulse of how I'm feeling when I ask students to respond to a question, has helped me be more aware of my frustration and increase my patience. This self-awareness has been key in noticing my emotional state and how it's contributing to my ability to meet my goal of wait time. Once that is done, I engage multiple strategies. I prepare, that is, I think about what could go wrong with my plan just ahead of a lesson that might be rushed. I practice the scenario, modifying my tone and pace of my words. I imagine myself as the conductor of an orchestra, varying pace, intensity and volume of my speech. I use an intervening moment with my class, simply by looking down before I ask a question. I use physiological techniques, striding up and down the classroom and critically, taking one, deep breath before I ask a question. And self-talk all the time, saying "wait, wait, wait" to myself.

OUTCOME Since I've increased my self-awareness around my feelings of impatience when students take some time to answer, the consistency of my wait time has gone up dramatically! It's amazing how something as small as noticing can play such a large role in improving my instruction. I've noticed students raising their hands more, and other students are more responsive when I cold call. Mapping my emotions made a huge difference because once I was aware of my emotions, I could then deploy effective strategies to move them to a more effective space. I do forget from time to time and when I slip up, I just smile to myself and know I'll nail it next time.

EI BLUEPRINT ANALYSIS This scenario highlights the importance of mapping one's emotions in order to pursue a goal. Accurate awareness of emotions allows us to be more intentional about how we Match our emotions to the task at hand or to Move our emotions to be more effective. Once the teacher was more cognizant of their emotional state, they were able to recognize the range of ways their emotions impacted their instructional strategies and shift the focus from their feelings during teaching, to students' feelings as they learn. Had they incorrectly mapped her emotions, they would have selected different Move strategies, perhaps sophisticated and multiple strategies, but strategies that would have proved ineffective. This teacher's high level of EI skill enabled them to correctly diagnose the challenge, in part by seeking input, and then successfully remediating it.

Effective regulation strategies the teacher used:

Prepare: Hope is not a strategy and, therefore, the teacher prepared for how things could play out and how their emotions could impact their goal of increasing wait time.

Intervening Moment: Intervening Moments may seem like space or dead air to others, but it was loud and busy inside the teacher's head when they took a moment without responding.

Self-talk: Self-talk takes mental space, and it also requires you to slow down a moment in order to actively engage in this self conversation. Our inner voice can help us focus.

Physiological: One deep breath, sometimes that is all it takes to hit the emotion reset button and slow us down.

GETTING THE LAST WORD (sworth)

EI LEVEL This teacher has an **average** level of EI skill.

LOWER	AVERAGE	HIGHER

BACKGROUND I've always loved literature. Chaucer, Shakespeare, Hemingway, I adore them all. When I became a high school English teacher last year I just knew my students would have the same passion for Dickens as I did (let's just say my initial assumptions were on the optimistic side). I felt so frustrated having to deal with all of these issues unrelated to the curriculum. This was supposed to be about literature. Instead, I had kids reading at a fourth grade level, behavior was off the wall and sonnets were not at the top of anyone's agenda. One morning after a particularly hard class, a young man named Austin, who had been tormenting me every day during first period looked me in the eye, and asked the question that still haunts me, "Mrs. Canon, you really don't like me do you? And in that moment of weakness I replied "No, I do not." He never spoke to me again. Sure, he stopped acting out, but it was like he disappeared. I felt so much shame at the interaction, that I haven't worked up the courage to address it. I know I am better than this.

GOAL To repair my relationship with Austin and to never repeat this behavior.

MAP *What are the emotions of you and others?* I feel so *ashamed* I spoke to Austin the way I did, yet at the same time I just feel like there are so many things stopping me from getting to what I really care about—teaching literature. I haven't really taken a lot of time to think about Austin's feelings. I guess I notice he's more withdrawn now in my class, so I know I have to do something about it, but there's a small part of me that's enjoying the respite. Still, I can do better. I need to sit down with Austin.

MATCH *What emotions are most helpful?* I was talking to my teacher mentor and she mapped an emotion I hadn't realized I had been feeling. I talked to her about trying to teach literature, and she reminded me my job was teaching students, and my classes were probably picking up on my sense of *resentment*. She reminded me that the first year of teaching was the hardest for her as well, and gave me some pointers to try out. I felt some of the weight lift off of my shoulders. As if I wasn't the only person who struggled with this. The conversation gave me a sense of *hope*. I started practicing my positive self-talk "I can be better, I will be better."

MEANING *What is the cause of these emotions?* I hadn't realized it until I had a conversation with my mentor that my *resentment* came from not wanting to feel like a failure. I knew I was good at analyzing literature, so I started blaming the kids for not appreciating the books I enjoyed in order to protect myself from the reality that I had a long way to go as a teacher. I guess Austin had better developed EI than I did because I now see he questioned me to confirm his suspicion that I cared more about Chaucer than I did about him.

MOVE *How will you sustain or move these emotions?* Reflecting on this situation helped remind me that a teacher who doesn't believe in her students' growth is not going to generate trust. I realize I wasn't the only teacher who struggled in their first year, which helped remove my *resentment*, and helped me forgive myself for not believing in my ability to grow as well. I've started using self-talk to look at every day as a growth opportunity and I felt ready to meet with Austin.

OUTCOME Owning up to my mistakes is hard, but I sat down with Austin first thing Monday and apologized for saying I didn't like him. I clarified that I didn't appreciate his behavior in my classroom, I knew he could do better and asked him what he needed from me to support his success in my class. He was aloof at first, but when he saw I really did want to make things better, he softened and I am hopeful our relationship will improve.

EI BLUEPRINT ANALYSIS This teacher has average EI skills. You know the importance of classroom management and yet it is a skill that eludes many educators. The hard skills of emotional intelligence provide a framework to help you with this critical task. In this situation, we see the importance of mapping one's emotions in order to pursue a goal. Once the teacher recognized they were holding a great deal of resentment because they feared failure, they were able to refocus and better attune to the emotions of the students. The teacher may have wished to explore in greater depth how the student felt before and after this interaction and the emotions they were generating in other students. Telling Austin they did not appreciate his behavior also off-loaded the issue onto the student when it was not clear whether he contributed in any way to the situation. Doing a bit of "emotional what-if" planning could help the teacher better prepare for classes and difficult interactions. The teacher's self-talk strategy helped improve their optimism and changed the tone in the classroom.

Effective regulation strategies the teacher used or could have used:

Self-talk: "I think I can, I think I can" sometimes can indeed work at effecting change. This teacher adopted a simple mantra as a reminder of what they aspire to be.

Express Concern: Telling students you care can make you vulnerable, but it also expresses your underlying and noble motivation to teach.

Select or Modify Situation: The teacher met with Austin Wednesday first period, a time they generally felt harried and more stressed than usual. Given she had a late night Tuesday, and a special meeting Wednesday afternoon, almost any other day would have been conducive to a more productive meeting.

RECOVERING FROM BURNOUT

EI LEVEL This teacher has an **average** level of EI skill.

LOWER	AVERAGE	HIGHER

BACKGROUND I have been teaching for decades and used to love teaching and feeling energized by my students. Over the past several months I've noticed I've lost my spark and quite honestly, I have a hard time getting out of bed in the morning. I may not be the first one out the door at the end of the day but I no longer linger after school and don't spend time in the lounge. Instead, I hang back and count the days I have left of school, like I did when I was in third grade. I am pretty sure I am suffering from burnout. What's worse is my students sense I'm not into teaching and they haven't been as engaged because they see I'm not either. I know this isn't fair to the students and I don't want to end my career this way with six months left in the school year.

GOAL To feel engaged in the classroom and increase the engagement and learning of my students.

MAP *What are the emotions of you and others?* I have felt burned out for 2 years and I am *exhausted*. In the classroom I frequently feel *agitated, frustrated, guilty* and at times, *sad*. I rarely feel the *joy* I used to feel earlier in my career. My students look downright *bored* and some are *irritated* with my lack of interest and low energy approach. I even think one or two are *worried* about me because they see how much I've changed—and not for the better.

MATCH *What emotions are most helpful?* Of course, I know how I am feeling is not helpful or useful for the situation. Here I have one more school year left and each day feels like a death march when I walk to class. At a minimum, I should be feeling some sense of interest and if possible, a little excitement in the classroom. I want my students to remember me in a positive way! I need to bring some energy to the classroom and re-energize my students.

MEANING *What is the cause of these emotions?* I have been in the classroom for 35 years. I started in my early 20's and taught grade school, then elementary school, before spending the last 25 years teaching high school kids. Kids have changed and I am tired of their antics. And, I've changed too. I don't have the patience I used to and I don't care for learning new technology, the constant testing and new initiatives. I need to hit my retirement target age and years of service in order to pay the bills so I can't just walk away. I don't blame my students for feeling the way they do. I would too if I had to spend 90 minutes with a grouchy teacher!

MOVE *How will you sustain or move these emotions?* By completing this Blueprint, it helped me see even more clearly, that I am not where I want to be. It is not healthy for me or my students and I must take action. There are many Move strategies I can use, and the most important ones are the long term ones—eating healthy, getting enough sleep, exercising, social support and mindfulness. Over the past year I've let all of these important activities take a back seat. From now on I am going to enlist the help of my family and friends in taking better care of myself. The other important strategy I am going to use is to modify my mood. I'll probably still head to school feeling down, but as I walk into the classroom I will remember to express a different emotion, to smile, to psych myself up for the day just like I did decades ago. Another strategy I will try is to re-appraise the situation, to take the perspective of my students, and provide them with the experience they need and will remember fondly. If I remember, I will practice appreciation and gratitude for what teaching has brought to my life and make sure I connect to each of my students personally.

OUTCOME Once I realized my behaviors weren't conducive to self-care, I began taking better care of myself, but it was short lived. Within a few weeks, I fell back into some of my familiar patterns and couldn't shake the burned out feeling. The good news is I was able to modify my mood by playing uplifting and motivating music before entering the classroom. Even my students noticed the positive shift and the classes became more engaging and fun. I did end up retiring at the end of the school year, and even though I was still exhausted, my students continued to learn and I felt better about retiring. I am enjoying my retirement and have re-engaged with the colleagues and friends I failed to make time for before. I am still working on long-term Move strategies, but I am so happy to have reconnected and re-established important relationships.

EI BLUEPRINT ANALYSIS This teacher has average EI skills. While the teacher did take action to change some of their behaviors, it didn't last very long. They began to exercise more and eat a healthier diet, but didn't take time to relax and unwind. The teacher wasn't sleeping well which caused them to be frequently exhausted. Even though they were partially successful in deploying long-term strategies, they were extremely successful in modifying their mood before entering the classroom. This made a "good enough" difference in the teacher's ability to keep everyone engaged in learning.

Effective regulation strategies the teacher used:

Long Term: Unfortunately, long term strategies are often the hardest to sustain. We start out with good intentions, then life takes over. The best way to implement change in behaviors is to enlist others in supporting us. Perhaps if they had asked their partner, friends and family for help with long term strategies, they would have been more successful in making lasting change. Long term strategies include getting seven hours of sleep, eating a healthy diet, frequent exercise, social support and some form of meditation, prayer, mindfulness or relaxation.

Modify Mood: People often ask the difference between a mood and an emotion. An emotion has an underlying cause, whereas a mood is nonspecific and usually not attributable to any one thing. Yes, the teacher had an underlying cause for feeling burned out, but was able to temporarily modify her mood as to not negatively impact her students. We know emotions are contagious and the teacher's behaviors caused the students to disengage. You need to be able to match your mood to the goal at hand and the teacher's goal was to ensure the students learned as much as possible. Therefore, using music to modify mood worked beautifully in this situation.

Relationships: One thing the teacher did, although in post-retirement, was to connect with others and re-establish relationships. Our social connections can be critical to our well-being. As we noted previously, had the teacher worked on long-term strategies while teaching, they might have had more success, or there would not have been such a sudden fade-out effect.

A BIG SHIFT IN TEACHING

EI LEVEL This teacher has an **average** level of EI skill.

LOWER	AVERAGE	HIGHER

BACKGROUND A complete transition to online learning? Are you kidding me? This is so stressful. Our principal met with us today informing us that we need to plan and deliver online lessons, which start in one week! I'm pretty sure my teacher education course did not cover this. It's hard enough motivating students in real life, now I have to do it online? How am I supposed to pay attention to this training when I am so stressed out? I need to figure out some strategies not only on how to shift to on-line learning, but also my emotions around it. Okay, I think I read in a book about emotional intelligence once on how I can use my emotions to facilitate problem solving. I think there are some Map, Match, Meaning and Move strategies that will be useful in this situation. And I really need to get going since our first teacher training is later today.

GOAL To remain open to online teaching training and then to create new ways to engage my students in learning.

MAP *What are the emotions of you and others?* I was feeling really *anxious* and *worried* about having to take this new approach to teaching. I haven't had a chance to think about others, but I would guess my students are feeling the same way about this huge shift, or perhaps they simply don't really care about any of this.

MATCH *What emotions are most helpful?* I read in my EI book that a small amount of anxiety can be motivating, but too much can be paralyzing. Worry can also be a useful emotion as it helps us pay more attention to details. However, I'd like to bring my anxiety and worry to a level that allows me to stay open and learn. I know my emotions are contagious and if I am overly anxious and worried, my students will feel it as well. Realistically, I don't want them to be panicked. Ideally, I want them to feel excited about new ways of learning!

MEANING *What is the cause of these emotions?* My first year of teaching is hard enough without having to learn a whole new approach. Classroom management was never my strong suit, and I'm really worried the online approach is going to be a disaster. If I focus too much on my anxiety, I won't be able to learn anything about how to do this! I know my students are struggling with not seeing their friends at school, and some have shared with me they are feeling worried online learning just won't be the same. I know them well enough that even though they complain about school, it's also a safe place for them when their home life becomes chaotic. Without daily support from me and the school, I worry about my students but feel hopeful everything will turn out all right.

MOVE *How will you sustain or move these emotions?* I really need to pay attention to this class but know being hyper anxious will not help me stay open. Therefore, when I notice myself thinking, "*I'll never get this.,*" I'm going to shift my thinking to "*This is an opportunity for me to improve my skills, how can I use these in the classroom to become a better teacher?,* and, "*I've mastered things like this in the past, I'm feeling optimistic I can do this too!*" I also know my students are struggling with this change in learning so I will start out with how we are in this together. Maybe we can use this as an opportunity. I want them to know I am here to support them and everything is going to be alright.

OUTCOME Having some emotional intelligence awareness reminded me how emotions can influence my attention. By becoming aware of my mixed emotions, I was able to be cognizant of how my thoughts impacted my feelings and how my feelings impacted my behaviors. By using self-talk, I became more present during the training. I took really good notes and heard information from other teachers who had successfully done this before that left me feeling encouraged. The next day I contacted my students to touch base and I could see their relief that I was there to support them and how much I cared about their wellbeing.

EI BLUEPRINT ANALYSIS Having re-read the emotional intelligence book helped the teacher, with average EI skills, understand how different emotions help facilitate different tasks. The teacher recognized their intense anxiety over online learning wouldn't be conducive to learning or applying new teaching strategies. Instead, they were able to map how they were feeling by paying attention to their thoughts and then shifting them to a slightly less unpleasant state to help them learn. The teacher was not as attuned to how students might feel and could have reflected more about how students might react. They were aware that anxiety can be helpful as it can focus our attention, something needed when we are learning new and difficult material. The teacher later used emotional connection as a strategy for moving their students' emotions from a place of worry, to a place of acceptance. Their hopefulness is encouraging, but at the same time may limit the teacher's awareness of future problems. Wishful thinking is something we all engage in, but oftentimes, it isn't the best Move strategy.

More effective regulation strategies the teacher could have used:

Self-talk: Self-talk comes in all forms and can be helpful or unhelpful. The teacher was thinking that switching to online learning was going to be a disaster and this thought led them to feel anxious. Fortunately, they realized how unhelpful this emotion was and shifted to more constructive self-talk, the inner voice that told them "I can do this," "I am a competent person" and "I really care about my students." This shift allowed the teacher to be more receptive to training and have a better outcome.

Emotional Connection: Emotions are how people connect and empathy is a way to build trust. Sometimes we forget how important it is, but when we imagine how others are feeling and reach out to them to acknowledge and validate their feelings, we build emotional connections. The teacher was able to put aside their feelings and place themself in their student's world. Because the teacher cared so much for their students, calling them individually came naturally and by doing so, helped them feel supported and less anxious so they were ready to learn and engage in new and exciting ways.

Relationships: New school or district-wide initiatives have one, universal positive: you have company. This teacher could have spoken with colleagues who are going through the same experience. Perhaps hearing how others were struggling and how some teachers were figuring it out would have helped to create a learning mode for this teacher.

CONFLICT IN THE CAFETERIA

EI LEVEL This teacher has a **higher** level of EI skill.

LOWER	AVERAGE	HIGHER

BACKGROUND Contrary to most teachers, lunch duty has always been my favorite part of the day and today is no different! I simply love watching students in their "natural habitat" negotiate problems amongst themselves, and the second grade cafeteria is the perfect time to watch these skills unfold. As I'm enjoying the familiar chatter, loud voices erupt at one of the tables. I quickly walk over to address the issue and from what I can tell, it looks like Gladys is making fun of Ray because he doesn't have a snack. I can feel my anger building because bullying is something I won't tolerate, especially at school. What I didn't know at the time was the real reason for her behavior—Gladys was excited about her mom packing her favorite snack and rather than share how she felt, she chose to pick on Ray.

GOAL To restore peace in the cafeteria and resolve the conflict between the two students.

MAP *What are the emotions of you and others?* I am *angry* Gladys is making fun of Ray. I've talked about and modeled the importance of empathy, and I'm *disappointed* Gladys is behaving this way. I'm also *sad* Ray is experiencing this type of interaction in our school. What does this say about our climate and culture? I can only imagine how Ray feels, perhaps *sad, angry and ashamed* for being picked on for not having a snack. Gladys is more difficult to figure out, but just seeing her and hearing a few words, one guess is she is feeling *exhilarated*.

MATCH *What emotions are most helpful?* Gladys should understand my anger at her behavior. She's committing an injustice! At the same time, while I want to teach her why it's important to feel empathy, my anger could cause her to shut down and become defensive. Therefore, I'm going to have to choose my words carefully. I also want to show her how much I care about the well-being of all the students. For Ray, I want him to feel safe and happy in our school and with adults who will make sure no one is mistreated. Thankfully, I've been trained in emotional intelligence so this process of reasoning about how to proceed is fluent and quick. By the time I walk over to the table, I'm clear I need to calm my anger and focus on my goal of restoring peace.

MEANING *What is the cause of these emotions?* I take great pride in the culture I've built in my classroom— it's part of my core identity as a teacher. I understand my disappointment and anger comes from the sense that I haven't done enough to prevent a situation like this. I wasn't sure why Gladys was acting the way she was and this had me at a disadvantage on how to resolve the issue. Therefore, I asked Gladys if we could go for a walk and talk about what was going on. I also told Ray I would talk with him later and before I left, let him know I was sorry for what happened and that no one in our school should be treated that way.

MOVE *How will you sustain or move these emotions?* From the moment I heard the disruption to the time I arrived at the table, I knew exactly how I was going to handle the situation. I know myself very well and disruptive behavior causes me to kick into action. Therefore, before speaking to the students, I took a moment to assess the situation. When I realized Gladys was bullying Ray, I felt anger building inside of me and disappointment that this behavior exists in our school. I knew if I was going to make this a teachable moment, I had to shift from anger to interest as to what caused Gladys to behave the way she did. This allowed me to remember my goal of using these teachable moments to support my students' social emotional development. I did share how upset and disappointed I was—not in her as a person—but how her behavior impacted Ray. As a result, rather than shut down, she opened up. It would have been easy to blame Gladys and had I done so, she in turn would have become angry at the injustice *I* was committing. By changing my emotion from anger to concern and support, she was able to share why she acted the way she did and I realized she didn't do it to hurt Ray's feelings. Once she realized what she did, she truly felt empathy for Ray and knew she needed to explain her behavior.

OUTCOME I pride myself in not forcing inauthentic apologies between students. My ability to move my emotions and keep my goal in mind helped to debrief the situation between Gladys and Ray first separately, and then together, resulting in Gladys recognizing the harm she inadvertently caused and repairing the relationship through an authentic apology. In addition, Gladys left with a larger toolkit in her toolbox when it comes to building and sustaining relationships. She now recognizes how her expressions impact others while at the same time she is able to express her own emotions more freely. If I wasn't well-trained in emotional intelligence, I may have never got to the root cause of the problem.

EI BLUEPRINT ANALYSIS The teacher possessed a high level of EI skill and used many emotion regulation strategies to resolve this situation. Students constantly watch and role model teachers' behaviors, and the most important emotions to manage when intervening in conflict, are your own. The teacher knew their emotional trigger (bullying) and took an intervening moment to recognize it and to turn their attention to the goal at hand (to restore peace and resolve conflict). Instead of acting in an angry manner (the feeling of anger is a signal and is often extremely appropriate, but lashing out is not) the teacher disrupted the situation by distracting the student by taking a walk rather than dealing with the situation at the table. This allowed both the teacher and student a few moments to reflect and not act in the moment. The teacher also modulated their tone and instead of conveying anger, the tone was one of care and empathy. The teacher was even able to convey disappointment and anger, but in a softer way so the student stayed more open to feedback. The student realized her behavior was hurtful and she wanted to apologize to the other student. She also was more relaxed and able to share the real reason for her behavior. The teacher validated how exciting getting a favorite snack can be and that it's ok to share how you're feeling with your friends. By leveraging her emotional intelligence skills, the teacher created a teachable moment out of a conflict.

Effective regulation strategies the teacher used:

Intervening Moment: When strong emotions grab us, our attention, thinking and behavior changes, and if the emotion is not on-point, it can distract us. In this scenario, the main emotion was anger. Anger is a difficult emotion to regulate and takes strong emotional intelligence skills to navigate. The teacher was able to recognize the emotion (Map) and knew it wasn't the right emotion to have a teachable moment (Match). It was at that moment the teacher paused to think about how they wanted to respond to the situation before speaking. By deploying this strategy, they were able to have a positive conversation and outcome.

Distraction: At times, distraction is an effective way to diffuse unpleasant emotions in yourself and others. The teacher distracted the student by going for a walk to discuss the issue. This allowed for a deeper conversation that may not have happened at the cafeteria table. Distraction should be used sparingly as it can be disruptive and delay getting to the bottom of the cause of the emotion (Meaning) and taking action to Move emotions to a better place to achieve the goal. It can also signal to others that you do not recognize their concerns.

Modulate Tone: We sometimes forget emotions are displayed in others ways such as through body language, tone of voice and facial expressions. The teacher was angry and could have raised their voice which most likely, would have led to the students raising their voices. Instead the teacher still expressed dissatisfaction, but in a lower tone and slower pace. You can use tone of voice to inspire, focus people's attention and motivate them. In this case, the teacher modulated their tone and the student became more receptive to the teacher, allowing the student to come up with a solution to the situation.

PUSHING MY BUTTONS

EI LEVEL This teacher has a **lower** level of EI skill.

LOWER	AVERAGE	HIGHER

BACKGROUND It's 8:45 AM and I just got my lesson going when Oscar strolls into my classroom late—and without a pass. Although I would never admit it out loud, I've struggled to find a way to connect with Oscar. He rarely comes to class on time, and when he does, he has difficulty following instructions the first time. The smell from his breakfast sandwich in his book bag starts to waft throughout the classroom as Oscar ambles to his seat and immediately asks for a pen to do his work. He *always* does this. I ignore him and think—*He had time to get a breakfast sandwich but no time to bring a pen?* He asks again more loudly and I remind him to raise his hand. Suddenly, Oscar gets up and walks out of the classroom. I call out—"I hope you're walking yourself to the principal's office!" Wow, that was not how I wanted to react and now my lesson plan is blown and learning has screeched to a halt. I can't help but wonder what I could have done differently, because having students walk out of my classroom isn't good for me, or the students.

GOAL To effectively handle my emotions and situations like these in the future.

MAP *What are the emotions of you and others?* To be honest, I feel *annoyed*. How could Oscar prioritize breakfast over getting to class on time and being prepared? I also felt *embarrassed* that Oscar just walked out of my class. It's apparent Oscar feels no *shame* or *embarrassment* for disrupting the class. How did Oscar feel? I'm not really sure and I am not sure attending to his feelings was the issue here, it was his behavior.

MATCH *What emotions are most helpful?* I was justified in terms of being annoyed. What emotions are more helpful? Maybe, maybe not, but being mad was a signal to me and to Oscar that he crossed a line. Maybe it shut me down a little, but it was Oscar's behavior which totally ruined my lesson plan for the class. I have no idea what emotions are helpful in this situation. All I know is Oscar should have never left the classroom. It makes me look like I can't handle my classroom.

MEANING *What is the cause of these emotions?* Oscar and I have a history and unfortunately, this isn't the first time we've clashed. I have every right to feel mad when students disrupt my class by being selfish and prioritizing breakfast over learning. He had no right to embarrass me by walking out. Instead of taking responsibility for his actions, he chose to leave the classroom just because I ignored him.

MOVE *How will you sustain or move these emotions?* I have every right to feel the way I do. I'm the teacher and Oscar disrupted my classroom. I don't see any benefit for modifying my emotions and eventually Oscar will get over it because he needs to graduate this year.

OUTCOME Oscar left the class abruptly and the lesson plan fell apart. I ended up feeling worse after he left and my class didn't get to learn what I had planned for that day. Even worse, my relationship with Oscar deteriorated even further.

EI BLUEPRINT ANALYSIS This was not the teacher's best day and unfortunately, they did not possess the level of emotional intelligence skills needed to successfully navigate the situation. Both teacher and student took the situation personally and communication (and learning) shut down. The situation started to unravel pretty quickly. Had the teacher utilized emotional intelligence, they may have perceived Oscar felt disrespected. Rather than labeling their own emotion as a generic "annoyed," they may have realized they felt indignant instead. The teacher's field of vision was narrowed as they were annoyed, angry and indignant. When Oscar was attacked—verbally—Oscar also likely felt increasingly trapped and his thinking became focused on protecting himself, not physically but emotionally. Oscar's self-talk is focused on the fact the teacher ignored him and then corrected him when he asked again for a pen without acknowledging his request. The teacher's self-talk is fueled by their feelings and focused on Oscar's prioritization of breakfast over getting to class on time and being prepared. This is compounded by Oscar's apparent lack of shame and urgency to follow the classroom routine. The teacher had a public situation where a student flouted his request and this may have added to their level of frustration and embarrassment. It's understandable, and many of us might feel the same way. However, had the teacher learned effective Move strategies, they might have avoided the situation.

Effective regulation strategies the teacher could have used:

Distraction: Instead of ignoring Oscar's late arrival, the teacher could have greeted Oscar upon entering the classroom. This would have created a positive bias between them and distracted the teacher from unpleasant feelings of indignation. Behavior influences emotions, just as emotions influence behavior. Behaving in prosocial ways, like saying "good morning" to all students when they enter the classroom creates positive emotions in both the greeter and the person receiving the greeting.

Reappraisal: Being aware of your thoughts and feelings creates opportunities to be more intentional about your interactions. Once the teacher becomes aware of the narrative in their mind (key terms like "always" or "never"), it should have triggered them to reappraise their thoughts. For example, when thinking *"He never has a pen,"* reframe it to *"Is there a time when he has brought a pen?"* Instead of thinking *"He's always late,"* reframing it to *"Is there an example where Oscar has been on time?"* And perhaps the best reappraisal being from *"I can't believe he is disrupting my class"* to *"I wonder if something happened that caused him to be late for my class?"* When you reappraise your thought process from deficit thinking to more positive thinking, it helps you see different possibilities and options to proceed.

Intervening Moment: Take a pause, just one or two seconds, take a breath, and then remind yourself of your goal. When the teacher felt indignation, they could have paused before they acted and asked, *"What am I trying to accomplish in this situation? How can I connect with Oscar at this moment?"* Grounding yourself in your goals helps guide your decisions towards more constructive outcomes. Instead of ignoring Oscar, the teacher could have acknowledged his arrival and centered themself in the goal of providing an enriching learning experience for all students.

Express a Different Emotion: Showing positive interest in Oscar and expressing happiness at seeing him, could have changed the teacher's feelings towards Oscar. It would not have taken a great deal of psychic energy to do so and it could have changed the underlying behavior. "Oscar, glad you are here," said in an upbeat manner, might have made a very small but important difference in the outcome.

ADMINISTRATOR BLUEPRINTS

Educational administration has unique challenges. The following EI Blueprints address common challenges administrators—and in one case teachers—face and how to use the Blueprint process to address these challenges. Administrators work closely with families and teachers and we include Blueprints which we hope you will find helpful in having constructive interactions and to form quality relationships with families and teachers.

PLEASE DON'T SUE ME!

EI LEVEL This assistant principal has an **average** level of EI skill.

LOWER	AVERAGE	HIGHER

BACKGROUND I've been an assistant principal for about 10 years. Recently, I was asked by my principal, to speak with a parent of a fourteen year old, Darren, who was receiving special education services for learning disabilities. I knew Darren; I had seen him around school with other kids and hadn't heard about any issues with him. The meeting sounded easy enough. Well, it turns out Darren's mom wanted to pull him out of any trips and all extracurricular activities because she was concerned Darren wasn't fitting in. I was really taken aback. The teachers in the triennial seemed to think he was doing great! Apparently over dinner, Darren had mentioned a minor altercation he had in school last week, and that's when Darren's mom decided she was considering filing a lawsuit. It was clear to me this wasn't going to be as easy as I thought. It was time for me to really put the emotional intelligence skills I had learned in a recent training to work.

GOAL My initial goal was to address and hopefully resolve the parent's issues and keep Darren in class, but my new goal was to not have a lawsuit!

MAP *What are the emotions of you and others?* I was initially *interested* and a little *curious* about the reason for the meeting. When Darren's mom came into my office she seemed *okay* and not at all *angry.* This all changed the moment she mentioned suing our school. I was really *surprised,* I mean I was blown away. What was *confusing,* was she related all of this in a pretty *calm* manner.

MATCH *What emotions are most helpful?* As I said, I was interested in what I was going to hear and I think this was nearly a perfect emotion to have in this open-ended situation. For the mom, too, my guess is her emotions matched the task at hand—to explain her views on how Darren was being treated and how upsetting this was to her family.

MEANING *What is the cause of these emotions?* Perhaps the phrase "This should be easy" should be eliminated from the vocabulary of assistant principals entirely! You never know what the day will bring or what a simple meeting like this might uncover. I was totally unprepared. Maybe I should have done a bit more due diligence, not by asking teachers "Everything okay with Darren?" which typically results in the standard reply "Yeah, everything's fine." If a parent calls for a meeting, it's usually not because they want to tell me how great things are going for their child. I was too laid back and did not predict how things could have turned out. It's not like we create our own bad luck by thinking about these things, it's more like what I used to do as a teacher before class; I had a little mental checklist to make sure I recalled what the lesson was, had my notes, did a quick rundown of who was in the class, made sure my computer was charged up and I had my reading glasses. It took less than a minute.

MOVE *How will you sustain or move these emotions?* After the initial shock, I stopped for a moment, looked down and took a deep breath, The voice inside my head said, *Darn! I really did not see that coming. Now what?* Those two seconds, I think that's all it was, let me hit the reset button. I was feeling pretty defensive but managed to eke out a "I am really sorry to hear that, I thought Darren was doing well. It sounds like you are concerned about how he is being treated by other students." I expressed concern, which was easy since I knew Darren a little bit and also liked him. The mom was still pretty calm, a lot more than I was and this helped de-escalate my inner tension. "Okay, okay, now what?" was my inner voice talking again, although a little less in panic mode. I told the mom I could see how this was really upsetting to her and to Darren. Rather than arguing with her, I agreed with her, at least how she felt about the situation. I knew there was no use arguing about it.

OUTCOME It turned out Darren's mom was very *anxious* about his well-being, which is not what I thought at first. She didn't want to restrict his opportunities as much as she wanted to feel like we cared about Darren as much as she did. I was surprised about the power of mapping her emotions, after I initially got it wrong, when I reflected them back to her. I picked this up in that EI training I took! I think once the mom realized I was not being difficult and actually cared, all of a sudden we went from talking about lawyers to talking about Darren's social skills and how we could work together to support him. I did not read her correctly, she wanted the best for her son, and I get that now. Instead of a lawsuit, we have a positive path ahead in support of Darren's development.

EI BLUEPRINT ANALYSIS This principal has average EI skills. This was a disaster waiting to happen but the assistant principal, once they realized what was going on, was able to pause and get back on track. It looks like the context of the meeting, and their initial read of Darren's mom was off, they did not Map her emotions as accurately as they could have and therefore, missed some critical data. The data could have signaled a real issue, it could have put the assistant principal on alert. Fortunately, the mom was honest and open from the beginning which allowed the assistant principal to pause and recover and end the conversation with a more constructive solution. Darren's mom wanted a solution to the problem and was advocating for her son. When the assistant principal finally realized this, and addressed the mom's concerns, it wasn't too late.

Effective regulation strategies the assistant principal used or could have used:

Intervening Moment + Physiological: Once you say it, you cannot unsay it and the assistant principal took a two-second pause before responding. Sometimes, that's all it takes. A few seconds won't always work to move your emotions but even a short, intervening moment can help you move the intensity or energy of the emotion down a notch or two. Combine that with even a single, deep breath and you can reset your perspective.

Express Concern: "How can I help?" Educators are helping professionals, that's why you signed up for this career. You can't always fix things, and your students, parents and colleagues aren't always looking for a solution, but asking what you can do for them, helps deescalate the situation.

Match and Validate: You'll see us suggest this strategy over and over. It's fairly straightforward and powerful at the same time. Darren's mom is entitled to her feelings about the situation and it is not our role, nor our right, to invalidate others' feelings.

TERRIBLE TIME TEAM TEACHING

EI LEVEL This teacher has a **lower** level of EI skill.

LOWER	AVERAGE	HIGHER

BACKGROUND I never really understood the purpose of Collaborative Team Teaching (CTT) classrooms. I mean, I know what they told us in my teacher prep courses—that a special education teacher and I would work together to support the needs of all students, including the ones with individualized education plans (IEP), but that's not what it is like in real life. I've been working with Amanda, who's my CTT teacher, and basically I send her my lesson plans the day before and she tells me they haven't been differentiated, and then in the class she just hangs out until I tell her to do something. I get it, she's fresh out of school, but I feel like I'm doing all the work here, and all I get in return is a larger class than I would've had by myself. It's gotten so frustrating that I've stopped sending her my lesson plan and just let her mill about the classroom doing whatever she wants during class. Hopefully, she will get the message. If not, I'm going to go complain to my principal and see if I can get a new teacher to work with.

GOAL Amanda has to go and ideally, she will go under her own power rather than having the principal do it. I just want to have my own classroom back. And if that cannot happen, I want someone who is not a burden on me and maybe even a little bit helpful at times.

MAP *What are the emotions of you and others?* I am basically *okay*, it's just that teaching is not as rewarding as it was before Amanda. I am not saying I always looked forward to coming to school, some days were worse and some better. I am also *frustrated* that I'm working so hard, while Amanda sits around doing what she wants. As for Amanda, who knows? She is pretty hard to read. I guess she is feeling *fine*, after all why not? She is young, just out of school, gets paid every month, doesn't do much at work, what's to complain about?

MATCH *What emotions are most helpful?* I am feeling what I am feeling, whether they are helpful or not, and just not sure if this matters right now. What would be helpful is to feel less stressed and less burdened by having to deal with a "collaborative" teacher who isn't being helpful. Maybe if Amanda felt super frustrated she would see what I have to deal with and ask for a transfer?

MEANING *What is the cause of these emotions?* I understand I can be somewhat set in my ways. And I understand the underlying rationale for collaborative teaching; in fact, it's worked out in the past for the most part. I have tried to be nice but Amanda is just not helpful and this is the source of my frustration.

MOVE *How will you sustain or move these emotions?* I will smile at her if she looks in my direction, but I won't say anything or encourage her in any way to interact with me. She'll get the lesson when I give it to her and if she complains about it, I will let her have it. I almost want her to come at me, that would give the excuse I need to tell her off. Unfortunately, she is just being polite and I have not been able to confront her.

OUTCOME Well apparently two weeks of disastrous team teaching isn't enough time to get sympathy from the principal and persuade them to change Amanda's teaching assignments. She asked me if I tried *talking* to Amanda, which I didn't because she should already know what to do! Sheesh, I guess I'm going to have to go tell Amanda why she isn't doing a good job since the principal won't.

EI BLUEPRINT ANALYSIS This Blueprint illustrates how a teacher with lower EI skills might handle this challenge. This situation went sideways for a few reasons. It started with bad data, that is, with problems mapping emotions of the classroom teacher and the collaborative teacher. Saying you are "okay", "fine" or "good" means very little. The teacher was frustrated and Amanda was likely feeling the same way. Frustration could be somewhat helpful to generate the interest in asking to have a productive discussion, as long as that frustration is kept at a lower level.

Effective regulation strategies the teacher could have used:

Reappraisal: If the teacher was at all motivated and cared to repair the situation, this would be a good start. Things may have worked out differently if the teacher considered, ever so briefly, the possibility that Amanda may have been experiencing personal challenges and by reacting differently, it may have humanized and strengthened the relationship.

Prepare: Again, this was a tough situation. We cannot predict the future, but we can prepare for what to expect before having a tough conversation. The teacher could have prepared for possible reactions from Amanda which may include surprise, anger, frustration or defensiveness. And perhaps, they could even anticipate positive responses such as interest, care and concern for making the relationship stronger.

Select/Modify Situation: Hallway conversations, or engaging in complex discussion between classes, probably isn't the best place to have a productive conversation. Take time to select when and where to have the conversation when you are at your best, perhaps before or after school, during an open period or on a specific day of the week.

Express Concern: This might have been a stretch for the teacher in this situation but we mention it anyway. If you struggle to see the perspective of the other person, it will be difficult to express concern in a genuine manner. Therefore, if you cannot do this and mean it, don't even try!

UNCOLLEGIAL COLLEAGUES

EI LEVEL This principal has a **higher** level of EI skill.

LOWER	AVERAGE	HIGHER

BACKGROUND Being a principal has taught me a lot about people. When I first became principal 10 years ago, I thought it was all about instructional techniques and observations. Now that I am a little more seasoned, I realize being a good principal is all about understanding the people who work for you. One other lesson I've learned is you must have a high level of emotional intelligence to be an effective administrator. I took a course about five years ago on emotional intelligence and it was the most important professional development (PD) I've had on leadership. Right now, I'm grappling with an issue involving one of my teachers, Jill, and a paraprofessional, Michelle, who can't seem to get along. Michelle, the para, has been in the classroom for about 15 years, and Jill is fresh out of college (and about twenty years younger). Michelle and I have known each other since I became principal, so when she came to me and said Jill was being disrespectful, I knew it was time to kick my emotional intelligence into high gear!

GOAL To help both Michelle and Jill feel heard and strengthen their relationship going forward.

MAP *What are the emotions of you and others?* I have some mild *anxiety* and am feeling *concern* and *anticipation* on how to resolve this situation. If Michelle is feeling disrespected, then I can imagine she must also be feeling some *irritation* and maybe even *sadness*. I am sensing Jill is somewhat *frustrated* when she tries to introduce new ideas into the classroom and Michelle doesn't ardently support them.

MATCH *What emotions are most helpful?* The emotions I am feeling are actually helpful to the situation. It is very concerning when two colleagues aren't getting along and is not healthy for our school. Frustration is probably not going to help either Michelle or Jill. I am hopeful Michelle and Jill will come into the meeting feeling interested in resolving the issue but also concerned and mildly anxious as they are being called into my office to discuss this matter with me.

MEANING *What is the cause of these emotions?* I get extremely concerned and anxious when two colleagues don't get along. Disrespect is not tolerated behavior and as principal, I'm concerned how their behaviors will impact their students and maybe spill over and impact colleagues. Michelle is an experienced educator and good at what she does. If she feels her voice is not being heard, it's reasonable to assume she feels irritation and perhaps sadness, and sees Jill as being disrespectful towards her. I know Jill is frustrated with Michelle because she has a lot of new ideas and she feels blocked from executing her ideas and lesson plans.

MOVE *How will you sustain or move these emotions?* My emotions are relevant and actually helpful for my meeting with Michelle and Jill. I will listen to both of them and remain objective so they feel heard. I will guide the discussion towards what they want the students to get out of their class, and how different styles and experience in the classroom actually make for a richer learning experience. I know they might express their feelings in a direct way, and I will breathe, listen and re-engage them around what they both want for their students. I will do my best to ensure they understand I am here to support them. I am hopeful they will realize they both want the same things and see that their current behaviors are not helpful to the students and to their mutual goal.

OUTCOME Michelle and Jill both felt I valued them personally and professionally. We were able to openly discuss the issue as they recognized their behaviors were hurting their ability to educate their students. They trusted my intentions and we left the meeting putting systems in place to help them define roles more effectively and create mutual goals for the students. I will continue to monitor the situation, but I am not naive enough to think one conversation has put this issue behind us. It will happen again, so I'll do a check in with them towards the end of the week, and weekly going forward.

EI BLUEPRINT ANALYSIS The principal handled the situation extremely well by using their high-level EI skills to address the issue. Instead of letting worry shut them down or place blame, they were able to stay focused on the goal of unifying the two teachers for the greater good of the students. By focusing on the goal or task at hand, staying open to all emotions and practicing effective emotional intelligence strategies, everyone left the meeting feeling pleasant and ready to move forward in a positive direction. The principal's justifiable concern that one meeting "cured" the problem is important to note—use your ability to predict the emotional future (affective forecasting) to remind you that ongoing intervention is often needed for these negatively charged situations. While we want to feel positive about these sorts of meetings, where people leave smiling, it's critical to consider the need for additional interventions.

Effective regulation strategies the principal used:

Match and Validate: It's important when resolving challenges to stay reflective and interested and to help others feel valued and heard. The principal took time in the beginning of the meeting to listen to both Michelle and Jill to get "their side" of the story. Instead of placing blame, taking sides or getting defensive, the principal validated how they were both feeling by focusing attention on both of them.

Emotional Connection: Once both teachers felt validated, the principal thanked them for their dedication to the students and how fortunate the kids were to have two wonderful teachers who bring different skill sets into the classroom. The principal reminded them of why they became teachers and asked them what they wanted for their students. Even though they have two different teaching styles, it was the same thing! The principal knew that by connecting emotionally to why they became teachers and what they wanted for their students, it wouldn't take long to come together to share ideas on how they could be a better and stronger team.

Physiological: During the conversation, the principal felt many emotions—pride, anxiety, concern and trust. Frequently throughout the discussion, when they felt unpleasant emotions, which would have increased their defensiveness and shut down on what was happening, the principal took deep breaths, relaxed their shoulders and nodded their head which helped them relax and stay open to some of the unpleasant feelings.

IT'S A DISCUSSION, NOT AN ARGUMENT: PROVIDING DIFFICULT FEEDBACK

EI LEVEL This principal has an **average** level of EI skill.

LOWER	AVERAGE	HIGHER

BACKGROUND I've never really been a confrontational person and giving teachers difficult feedback is a skill I've been working on since becoming a principal last year. I've tried the sandwich method—you know, starting with a strength, moving to a need, and ending with a strength. Unfortunately, what this means for me is I mask the issue by not focusing on the main area of improvement. Even worse, my school is on a state watch list for academics and my superintendent expects instruction to improve yesterday! It's gotten to the point where I can't tell who's more anxious about observing the classroom, me or the teacher. I've also noticed the more I show nervousness when giving feedback, the more pushback I get from the teacher which takes precious time away from discussing what really matters—the teacher's instructional techniques. After my last disastrous encounter providing teacher feedback, I reached out to another principal I really respect and they shared some tips they learned over the years on how to deal with this situation using the skills of emotional intelligence.

GOAL To manage my anxiety and provide effective teacher feedback.

MAP *What are the emotions of you and others?* I was really good at instruction as a teacher, but adults are a lot different than kids. Sometimes I wish I could just go back to working with kids…but I know this school can benefit from my experience and knowledge. I just feel so *anxious* when there's tension. One teacher even started to feel *sad* and cry during one feedback session…and I hadn't even gotten to the most unpleasant part. I sense my teachers get *frustrated* when I'm unable to provide helpful feedback, which sends my anxiety through the roof.

MATCH *What emotions are most helpful?* Instead of feeling anxious I want to feel confident and warm and kind. I know my feedback is well-grounded and notice that when I'm more confident, my teachers incorporate my feedback more readily. I want my teachers to feel interested in the feedback and stay open so we can identify action steps for improvement.

MEANING *What is the cause of these emotions?* Adults are different from kids. I know this should seem obvious, but I'm still getting used to it. One teacher I had was really struggling with classroom management. I gave him some feedback and he just looked at me and told me my suggested technique wasn't going to work—even though I'd been successfully using the same technique during my ten years as a teacher, teaching the same grade! When I begin to think about unpleasant feedback scenarios, I lose confidence and start to feel more anxious. I can understand why the teachers may feel frustrated, or perhaps disappointed, when I'm unable to articulate what I am trying to say clearly because of my nervousness.

MOVE *How will you sustain or move these emotions?* I explained my situation to a friend who was a principal at another school and she told me I should take time to notice my body when I get anxious and intentionally relax different parts while focusing on breathing. She called them physiological techniques. As I started paying more attention to my body, I realized I was gnashing my teeth and curling my toes when I started to think about these feedback meetings. Just being aware of these cues allowed me to unclench my jaw and unroll my toes and strangely, my feelings of anxiety lessened. It's like my body and my feelings were linked. Another tip she gave me was to take 5-10 minutes before the meeting to get in the right mood.

Good advice, but that was not going to work given I don't have 5 or 10 extra minutes before each meeting! Still another idea she had was to change how I felt by expressing a different feeling. Therefore, if I wanted to feel a little more confident, I could simply express some confidence and smile that confident smile. That I could do! It doesn't take a lot of practice or time to smile. With all of this, I still did not feel completely confident but I'm definitely less anxious.

OUTCOME It's amazing how just noticing my body has helped me feel more in control of my anxiety. It's not perfect, and I still don't always feel the confidence I know my expertise deserves, but I don't shut down when I feel anxious. It's like I'm ready for it, and moving my body helps me move my emotional state. I ran into my friend recently and was pleased to tell her I'm getting better at providing constructive feedback. I monitor my body, breathe deeply, get into the right mood and lately, I feel my teachers are trusting my feedback and more importantly, their instruction continues to improve.

EI BLUEPRINT ANALYSIS Being emotionally intelligent begins with first noticing emotions within the body as they happen. The principal, whose EI skills are average, recognized anxiousness by labeling their feelings but hadn't noticed where it was showing up in their body. The principal contacted a colleague for advice, a helpful Move emotions strategy itself. The colleague offered ideas for not only noticing anxiety in their body, but ways to practice modifying their mood. Each of us has "go to" methods for pumping ourselves up or bringing our mood down. The key is to match the emotion to the task at hand, which the principal was able to do. These strategies helped them reduce their anxiety and enabled them to provide effective feedback. We also have a hypothesis: recall the principal said he was not a "confrontational person" and we wonder whether their anxiety caused them to view feedback as confrontational. By reducing their anxiety and increasing confidence, the principal was able to approach feedback in a more constructive manner.

Effective regulation strategies the principal used:

Physiological: Before humans developed language, and as seen in most of the animal kingdom, the only way to communicate emotions was through body language. Since much of these processes occur at the subconscious level, becoming aware of how your body is reacting to events helps move the experiences from the unconscious parts of processing, to the more conscious areas of the brain where things like intention, effortful control and abstract reasoning lie. This progression from unawareness to awareness helps develop a sense of control over the emotional state and mirrors the Map, Match, Meaning and Move approach detailed in this book.

Modify Mood: When facing unpleasant emotions, most people want to fix the problem as quickly as possible rather than sit with the discomfort. However, when you recognize the emotion within your body (Map), you can then decide what emotion is more helpful (Match) and then modify your mood to get to the right emotional state. It does take practice to notice emotions, but doing periodic body scans and getting into the right mood, especially before important meetings, can really help people achieve better outcomes.

Express a Different Emotion: The principal tried smiling to reduce anxiety and increase confidence. Although similar to modifying your mood, expressing a different emotion is a specific strategy where you select the desired emotion and express it. The principal wasn't denying how they felt, they were changing it in a proactive and constructive manner.

PARENTS BEHAVING BADLY

EI LEVEL This principal has a **lower** level of EI skill.

LOWER	AVERAGE	HIGHER

BACKGROUND It's days like this that makes my job as a principal difficult. Last week, two of my students had a fight in the hallway stemming from an issue on social media. Our dean conducted a mediation with the girls, but the parents insisted on meeting each other. Normally, I wouldn't do this, but it looked like the parents were taking to social media, saying bad things about each other, and prolonging the conflict between the girls. In fact, it was the girls themselves who were trying to help their parents resolve the issue. I was thinking, *why can't these parents just get it together?* Well, I brought the parents in and let them have it! I gave them my best lecture as to how we expect parents to behave. I even gave them my go-to line: "You should be *ashamed* of yourselves, you are the adults!" For some reason this didn't go over very well, and soon I had a shouting match in my office. Even worse, I had to call security to have the parents physically removed.

GOAL To resolve the conflict between two parents, or at least to get the parents to stop attacking each other on social media.

MAP *What are the emotions of you and others?* Why can't these parents be better role models for our kids? It's hard enough I have to do my job, but I have to teach the parents too? I rarely feel this level of being *ticked off* about parent behavior but I just feel like they need to understand what we expect in my school. I really have no idea how these parents are feeling other than they are *super angry* and honestly,

I am not sure I even care. I shouldn't have to spend my valuable time mediating a parental conflict outside of school.

MATCH *What emotions are most helpful?* I'm pretty sure when the parents recognize the quality of our school, and the superiority of my approach, they'll understand where I'm coming from. And, I'm pretty sure my emotions are perfectly matched to the task at hand (although I haven't really given it that much thought).

MEANING *What is the cause of these emotions?* I'm not sure it's my job to figure out why parents do what they do. Our school is one of the top schools in the state! It's bad enough we had a fight in our hallways, but for our parents to be behaving like this. I just don't have time for this sort of thing at my level and it's no wonder I feel the way I do about the parents.

MOVE *How will you sustain or move these emotions?* How I feel is how I feel and I have little need to justify myself. It's also up to the parents to manage their own emotions, that is not my role. They need to calm down and realize they are making things a lot worse. I don't really care about the parents' emotions because if their kids are going to be in my school, everyone better get their act together.

OUTCOME The parents and I met to discuss the issue and I let them know how abhorrent their behavior was and that it had to stop immediately. I was forceful and direct, but very professional, respectful and calm, just stating the facts. Instead of listening to what I had to say, they both got defensive and used abusive language. So much so, I had to have security escort them out of the building. I still don't really understand how things got so out of hand. I guess some people are just difficult. The problem did finally get resolved, when the parents removed their children from the school. I felt badly for my students but at least we no longer have to deal with the issue!

EI BLUEPRINT ANALYSIS The principal, whose EI skills are in the lower range, notes they could not imagine what the parents were feeling at the time. It takes some skill at Mapping emotions to detect emotions which are subtle, but the principal seemed to miss cues for emotions which were expressed fairly directly—and loudly. Had someone else observed the meeting, they would have recognized the *contempt* each parent had for the other and the *anger* both sets of parents had toward the principal. When we struggle to apply our emotional intelligence skills, conflict can often escalate. Instead of identifying constructive approaches to problem solving, disagreements can get to the point of confrontation, abusive language and at times, violent behavior. The principal did not take the time to match their emotions to the task and came off as arrogant, making it less likely for them to reach their goal of coming to consensus. Nor was there an attempt to Move emotion as the principal thought the displayed emotions were the right ones. Additionally, the principal struggled to identify the emotions of the parents and was unable to pivot when the approach was ineffective. Part of the problem was the principal was not even aware how the meeting was going and could not predict how the parents would react. Ideally, the principal could have invited the dean or another staff member to compensate for the principal's difficulty in mapping emotions. The principal also could have engaged in some emotional what-if planning with the dean or simply turned to the dean to run the meeting. Unfortunately, when people are low in EI, it is unlikely they will reach out for assistance.

Effective regulation strategies the principal could have used:

Reappraisal: Being aware of your thoughts and feelings creates opportunities for you to be more intentional about your interactions. If the principal had tried to find the meaning behind the parent's emotions, they would have been more aware the narrative in his mind was saying "Why can't these parents just get it together?" and instead used reappraisal by asking "What's happening with these parents to cause this behavior?" By being curious instead of contemptuous most likely would have resulted in a more positive outcome.

Self-talk: When the principal saw conflict arise, using self-talk to remind them of the goal of helping the parents come to a consensus would have helped the principal focus on the goal rather than attacking the parents. Self-talk helps shift the brain from shutting down, to a place of problem solving. Another approach the principal could have used was to actualize self-talk by writing down their goal in order to help cue motivational self-talk towards the preferred outcome. By focusing on the goal of wanting the parents' children to get the best education possible, it would help move them into a more neutral, if not positive, place for a productive discussion.

Match and Validate: The parents were obviously upset based on the social media posts and the meeting. When people feel anger or contempt, it can get personal. The principal could have taken time to hear both sides of the story and validate the parents' feelings. Most people, once heard and validated, will become open to possibilities and problem solving. Had the principal used this approach, perhaps there would have been a more positive outcome.

GIVING THE GIFT OF (UNWANTED) FEEDBACK

EI LEVEL This principal has an **average** (mixed) level of EI skill.

LOWER	AVERAGE	HIGHER

BACKGROUND Jesse is in his second year of teaching middle-school science and believes he is a really great teacher, even indispensable. Jesse has a number of strengths including excellent content knowledge and a passion for science. But I also feel he has some unpleasant traits such as constantly seeking praise, not working well with others and at times, balking at making changes to his teaching style. All this would be acceptable, albeit not desirable in our school, but now Jesse is becoming a bit disruptive in teacher meetings and some lessons I recently observed have been sub-par. I expect more from our teachers and from Jesse. As principal, I know it's time for a conversation to discuss the situation, but I'm a little concerned with how well my feedback will be received.

GOAL Understand the reasons for Jesse's behavior, to provide Jesse with candid feedback and help Jesse reach his career, and our school's, goals.

MAP *What are the emotions of you and others?* I am feeling *frustrated* and *annoyed* with Jesse. I have bent over backwards trying to give him advice and it is falling on deaf ears. I believe Jesse feels *frustrated* and perhaps *disappointed* he hasn't been recognized or appreciated. Jesse may feel I don't value his work or care about him—but that's just a guess.

MATCH *What emotions are most helpful?* My frustration is not helpful at this time. I need to remember Jesse is passionate about the subject work, wants to do a good job and wants some recognition. Jesse's recent behavior of being abrupt, not sharing important information, missing a deadline and showing his aggravation in the classroom is having a negative impact on his students and peers. I want to move Jesse from frustration to a more neutral state so he is less defensive and more open to having an honest discussion.

MEANING *What is the cause of these emotions?* I have tried giving Jesse advice many times and he isn't listening to me. I am getting more frustrated by Jesse's behavior and part of me doesn't want to even bother. However, although I haven't been able to spend much time with Jesse lately, I know Jesse has been under a lot of pressure both in and out of school. Jesse is a new parent and maybe that's a problem, although he hasn't said anything. We all want feedback as teachers so I think he will be fairly open this time since he must realize the situation has not gotten any better.

MOVE *How will you sustain or move these emotions?* During the meeting I will make sure to ask about the baby, the family, Jesse's work goals, and what he wants in terms of career and the school. Based on the answers to these questions, I will ask how I can better support reaching these goals. I will also be ready and instead of quickly feeling overwhelmed if Jesse expresses frustration or becomes defensive, I will stay open by taking a moment to breathe, reappraise the situation and then ask questions to gain greater understanding. I will show empathy, ask for Jesse's opinion, share my goals and how I am here to support him. Even better, I'll prepare for our meeting by taking deep breaths and have some phrases ready such as, "I can see how someone might feel that way" and "How can I help you?" If Jesse begins to get angry and loses focus, I'll try a different question. I'll remind Jesse of the goal for our conversation—that I am here to support him. I will practice deep listening and try to understand Jesse's perspective. If the conversation begins to go badly, we will take a break and re-engage later.

OUTCOME Jesse was really surprised to find out why I wanted to meet and I guess I was surprised he didn't know why we were meeting. At first, Jesse wasn't listening and became defensive. I started to get defensive as well and had to remind myself of the goal for our conversation. I took that intervening moment, that one deep breath which calmed me, and slowed by speech and softened my voice. Eventually, Jesse understood I cared about his future and him as a person and he started to relax. Jesse shared the stresses of home and the need to succeed at work. Jesse didn't realize the impact his behavior was having on colleagues or the classroom, believing that his emotion suppression was working quite well. Jesse shared his desire to be a great teacher and thanked me for the understanding and support I showed during our conversation. I added some additional concrete emotion management suggestions, reviewed an upcoming lesson, and expressed I was there to support him. It was an emotionally tiring interaction, but at least it felt constructive and productive. Even though Jesse continues to struggle with his colleagues, his in-class behavior has greatly improved.

EI BLUEPRINT ANALYSIS The principal had a mix of EI skills, slightly lower for Meaning and higher for Move. While he knew the conversation with Jesse was going to be a difficult one he had not really engaged in solid emotion "what-if" planning. Certainly, engaging in solid Meaning of emotion planning would have better prepared the principal. For example, knowing Jesse was stressed, the principal should have considered how the changed family situation was contributing to Jesse's negative behaviors. Hoping Jesse would become more open to feedback was also naive. Fortunately, the principal practiced solid Move strategies allowing for a more productive conversation and positive outcome.

Effective regulation strategies the principal used:

Match and Validate: The first ability of emotional intelligence is to accurately identify emotions. It takes practice to accurately identify someone's emotions and therefore, important to verify what emotions are being experienced before moving forward with the discussion. If the principal was inaccurate, or didn't ask how the other person was feeling, the conversation might have taken a different turn. However, the principal was correct and raised Jesse's awareness of what impact his emotions were having on his colleagues and students.

Reappraise: It's easy to fall for first impressions and the principal could have assumed Jesse was behaving poorly on purpose. Instead, the principal took time to look at the situation from different perspectives asking, "What else is happening in Jesse's life that could be causing them to act this way? Maybe he is unaware how he is coming across?" By reappraising the situation, the principal was able to see new possibilities on why Jesse was behaving so poorly.

Emotional Connection: Instead of getting angry about Jesse's behavior, the principal showed empathy, care and concern. This strategy helps build trust and allows the other person to be more open to feedback. Throughout the meeting, the principal practiced deep breathing, which is just one of many physiological strategies to reduce tension.

Express Concern: Most people become defensive when receiving feedback. Instead of focusing on Jesse's negative behaviors, the principal instead focused on Jesse as a person and expressed genuine concern for what he is experiencing. Showing care and concern for others helps form an emotional connection that builds trust.

PART THREE

Build Your Own
Emotional Intelligence Blueprint

Our Blueprints cover a wide range of common situations and challenges, but they will never reflect your *exact* situation. The Blueprint is a simple tool in principle, but like most simple ideas, it's difficult to apply well and consistently. To help you improve your instructional and leadership practices, we will walk you through the process for creating your own Emotional Intelligence Blueprint. By using the Blueprint, you can see challenges from different angles, by taking different perspectives and being reflective about how the parties in the situation felt and how these feelings influenced their thinking and behaviors.

We begin the Blueprint process with your outcome and goal in mind, so by the end of the Blueprint, you know what actions to take to resolve your challenge in the most emotionally intelligent manner possible. We provide you with multiple questions for each Blueprint step to help walk you through the process. There is no need to use all of the questions; they are provided as a way to structure your thinking and approach when constructing your own Blueprint.

The Blueprint Steps

With practice, you will develop your own process, but until then, we've found the following steps to be helpful and productive when creating a Blueprint.

1. Indicate your desired goal or outcome.

2. Map the emotions of the key people involved.

3. Match the emotions to the task or goal.

4. Determine Meaning of emotions for all parties and conduct what-if analyses.

5. Move emotions strategies for all people involved.

6. Conduct an after-action review to get feedback and enhance EI skills.

Step 1, Let's Start at the Very Beginning: The Desired Goal or Outcome

The Blueprint process is helpful when addressing challenges, but we hope you will use it prospectively to enhance your instruction and leadership. When we are faced with problems it's human nature to want to fix it as soon as possible so it goes away. Often we focus on how we are feeling, and the discomfort of experiencing unpleasant emotions pushes us to either ignore the situation, or quickly resolve it, even if we don't have a permanent or better solution. Therefore, it is important to begin the Blueprint not with the problem or challenge, but with the outcome and goal you want to achieve. This shift from problem solving to exploration of the situation helps open us up to other possibilities and ways of thinking.

To begin the Blueprint, try being as objective as possible, as if you're looking at it through the lens of a researcher or third party. Objectivity helps you view challenges with more neutrality and detachment and allows more helpful emotions to emerge which are important when analyzing difficult situations.

Desired Outcome/Goal Questions:
- What do I want out of this situation?
- When this situation is resolved, what changes do I want to see in behaviors and thinking?
- What outcomes will I see when these changes happen?
- What goals will we achieve?
- What are the obstacles to achieving this outcome?

- What do I worry may happen?
- How can this negative outcome be prevented?
- What role can I play in achieving the best possible outcome?
- Who can assist me with this desired outcome?

Step 2, Map Emotions

Once the goal and desired outcome is identified, next examine the emotions you and others are feeling at this moment. This is where emotional intelligence begins—being able to accurately identify emotions in yourself and in others. Take a moment to think of your current challenge and see what emotions bubble up. Usually when we complete a Blueprint it is because we are experiencing unpleasant emotions such as sadness, anger, boredom, frustration, loathing, etc. Do a body scan and notice what is happening in your body and in your thoughts. Write down every emotion you are feeling regarding the situation—and feel free to note where in your body you are feeling them.

Now we move on to how others are feeling. Your situation may involve one person, several people or a whole group of people. Take a moment to identify all of the emotions you've noticed in others. It is possible you could be wrong in identifying the other person's emotions because they are hiding their true feelings, or you may not be strong in this area of emotional intelligence. Regardless, write down what you believe the other person is feeling about this situation.

Map Questions:

- *How do you feel about your challenge now?*
- *How are you expressing your emotions related to this situation?*
- *How are others feeling about this challenge?*
- *How are others expressing their emotions related to this situation?*
- *How certain are you that you accurately mapped the other person's emotions?*
- *How might you be able to confirm your accuracy?*

- *How did you feel during this interaction? (Answer this question if you are doing a post conversation analysis.)*

Step 3, Match Emotions

Next, we move on to the second ability of emotional intelligence—the ability to Match the emotion to the goal or task at hand. As we noted earlier, research suggests certain emotions can facilitate certain tasks and problem solving. For example, if you want to have an end of school celebration, the emotions of joy, happiness and contentment are perfect for this occasion. And, if you have a looming deadline for an important project, perhaps the best emotions to achieve this task is anxiety, worry or sadness. When assessing your challenge, determine which emotions would be best suited to accomplishing your goal or the task at hand. This is not how you and others feel about the task—the question is, which emotion(s) can help with the task?

Match Questions:

- *Did it help you to feel this way? Why or why not?*
- *Which emotions would have been most helpful to address this issue?*
- *How much attention did you direct to the problem?*
- *Did your feelings guide you in the right direction? Did you ignore them or pay attention to your gut feel?*
- *Were you able to feel what the other person was feeling? Did you connect with them? To what degree? How do you know?*
- *How did the other person feel and think? How do you know?*
- *What is your guess as to the extent of the other person's connection with you?*

Step 4, Meaning of Emotions

Before taking action to Move your emotion to a more helpful one, it's important to get to the root cause of why you and others are feeling these emotions. If you skip this part of the Blueprint, you can go into problem solving mode without first addressing the underlying cause. Ask yourself, "Why do I and others feel the way we do? What happened to make me and others feel the way we do?" When we do this reflective work it allows us to understand the real meaning of emotions. And, it allows you to better understand the other person and see things from their perspective—or not! Finding the cause of emotions often leads to a better understanding of yourself and others. Determining the possible trajectory of the emotions you and others may experience is also critical as this allows you to predict how things could go wrong in unpleasantly charged situations.

Meaning Questions:

- *Why did you feel this way?*
- *What were the underlying causes for you?*
- *Why did the other feel the way they felt?*
- *What were the causes for their emotions?*
- *How were you feeling before this happened?*
- *How did your feelings change, and why?*
- *How did the other person's feeling change? Why?*
- *Can you list specific emotions you and the other person felt? (List specific words.)*

Step 5, Move Emotions

Once you have acquired good emotional data by applying the first three abilities of emotional intelligence, you can now decide how to Move the emotions, the fourth emotional intelligence ability, to effectively achieve your outcome. It takes conscious attention and skill just to maintain emotions and even if all is well, be vigilant and actively keep things moving along, as emotions can change, and often do. Up until now you have been thinking of your challenge, the emotions you and others are experiencing, whether or not these emotions are helpful and what caused these emotions to arise. And while all of these steps are important, it now requires you to take action to move your emotions to a place best suited to resolve the issue at hand. Once you know what emotions are more helpful, and identify the root cause, you can use various emotion management strategies to move your emotions and those of others. What strategy will help you and others reach the optimal emotions to achieve the goals and outcomes you desire?

There are a wide variety of strategies you can use as outlined in Part One of this book. After reviewing all of the strategies for you and others, select the strategies you feel will work best for your situation.

Move Questions

- *What are your feelings telling you about this situation?*
- *What strategies will you use to Move your emotions?*
- *What strategies will you use to Move others' emotions?*
- *How effective were the strategies you selected? What could be improved?*
- *Were there strategies you could have used instead or in addition to these? (Refer to the list in Part One.)*
- *How effective were the strategies you used for others? What could be improved?*
- *Were there strategies you could have used instead of or in addition to these? (Refer to the list in Part One.)*

Step 6, How Did It Go? Did you achieve your outcome or goal?

Things don't always work out how we planned. It's possible you achieved your desired outcome using these steps. Or, you could have achieved your desired outcome by changing the plan in real time. It's also possible something could have happened that prevented you from achieving your goal. Regardless of the outcome, it helps to refine your skills by getting feedback on how the goal was achieved and how people are feeling. If people aren't feeling positive about the outcome, chances are the issue will resurface. Take some time for a Blueprint after-action review. These questions are for you, but ideally you will ask a trusted colleague these questions and listen to the answers.

Outcome and Analysis Questions:

- *What happened as a result of the interaction?*

- *What did you want to happen?*
- *What worked well?*
- *What could you have done differently?*
- *Was there a better way to have handled it?*
- *How satisfied were you with the outcome?*
- *How satisfied do you think the other person was with the outcome? How do you know?*
- *Are there any actions you could take now to result in a more productive outcome?*
- *What did you do that you would do again in a similar situation?*
- *What lessons did you learn? And what did the other person learn?*
- *How are you feeling now about the situation? Others?*
- *Do the emotions you are others are feeling set you up to continue positive working relationships?*

A Structured Approach to Building Your Own Blueprint

Some of us struggle with such broad, open-ended questions, especially as we develop the vocabulary of emotional intelligence and hone our skills. We've found that it's oftentimes easier to use a more structured approach to creating Blueprints. In this section, we provide you with a suggested checklist to help guide you through the process.

Step 1, Desired Goal:

First, consider your goal or objective and record it. Next, check the box which most closely matches your goal[20]. Then, indicate what the other person's objective is and how you arrived at this conclusion.

---

20 Based on Sternberg & Dobson (1987).

Desired Outcome or Goal	
What is your goal or objective?	Your goal:
Which of these best match your objective or goal?	• A: Get other party to alter their position through assertion, criticism and coercion • B: Do not dwell on the issue, move past the issue and forget it • C: Negotiate, understand and persuade
What is the other person's goal or objective? How do you know?	Other person's goal and how I know:

Note that the strategies in the second column are oftentimes labeled confrontation (A), avoidance (B) and collaboration (C), respectively. In general, the EI Blueprint is based on collaborative strategies (C).

Step 2, Map Emotions:
Next, indicate the emotions experienced by the person or people involved, including you (use initials for each person).

EMOTION	Do not feel ← → Strongly feel		
ANGER	☐ No	☐ Irritated	☐ Frustrated	☐ Angry
SADNESS	☐ No	☐ Down	☐ Sad	☐ Depressed
SURPRISE	☐ No	☐ Curious	☐ Surprised	☐ Shocked
SHAME	☐ No	☐ Uncomfortable	☐ Embarrassed	☐ Ashamed
FEAR	☐ No	☐ Concern	☐ Worried	☐ Afraid

EMOTION	Do not feel ← → Strongly feel			
PRIDE	☐ No	☐ Confident	☐ Assured	☐ Proud
HAPPINESS	☐ No	☐ Content	☐ Happy	☐ Joyous
EXCITEMENT	☐ No	☐ Interested	☐ Excited	☐ Enthusiastic
How sure are you about the emotions you identified? How were these emotions expressed?				

Step 3, Match Emotions:

Next, indicate the influence these emotions had on each person. Place their initials in the appropriate block.

← Influence on Thinking →										
Focused on details	☐	☐	☐	☐	☐	☐	☐	☐	☐	Big picture
Accepting	☐	☐	☐	☐	☐	☐	☐	☐	☐	Looking for a fight
Closed to ideas	☐	☐	☐	☐	☐	☐	☐	☐	☐	Open to new ideas
Sees negatives	☐	☐	☐	☐	☐	☐	☐	☐	☐	Sees positives
Fixed opinion	☐	☐	☐	☐	☐	☐	☐	☐	☐	Easily persuaded
Slow, thoughtful	☐	☐	☐	☐	☐	☐	☐	☐	☐	Quick to decide
Closed to bad news	☐	☐	☐	☐	☐	☐	☐	☐	☐	Open to bad news

Now, indicate the extent of a felt connection between the people in this situation and what the feelings were like; that is, describe the physical sensation each person experienced. Begin with the intensity of the emotional connection and then the overall feeling of the relationship. If there are more than two people involved, you can add them (feel free to include people's real name).

Relationship	Emotional Connection	Overall Feeling
Person 1's emotional connection with Person 2	[ ] [ ] [ ] [ ] [ ] Weak Moderate Strong	Warm . . . . Cold Relaxed . . . . Tense Sweet . . . . Bitter
Person 2's emotional connection with Person 1	[ ] [ ] [ ] [ ] [ ] Weak Moderate Strong	Warm . . . . Cold Relaxed . . . . Tense Sweet . . . . Bitter

Step 4, Meaning of Emotions:
Next, indicate the underlying causes of these emotions.

Meaning of Emotions		
To what extent are these feelings (Map) due to a mood (no major underlying event or cause) or to your current situation (Match)?	☐ Mostly Mood	☐ Both	☐ Mostly Situation
To what extent are the feelings of the other person due to a mood or to the current situation?	☐ Mostly Mood	☐ Both	☐ Mostly Situation
How did/will your emotions or feelings change if the situation continues?	☐ Decrease	☐ Same	☐ Increase
How did/will the other person's emotions or feelings change if the situation continues?	☐ Decrease	☐ Same	☐ Increase
What else do you think is the underlying cause of these emotions?		

Emotions have an identifiable cause and being clear about the underlying cause—a double check of sorts—can help you better plan to address the situation. Next, we consider the underlying theme for basic emotions.

Causes of Emotions—You

Now consider the *underlying* theme or cause of the main emotions present in this situation for **you**. Indicate the exact event or cause for the emotion(s) experienced in this situation:

Anger	Obstacle or injustice	
Surprise	Unexpected Event	
Sadness	A loss	
Fear	Impending Threat	
Disgust	Norms violated	
Happiness	Gain something of value	

Causes of Emotions—Other Person

Now consider the *underlying* theme or cause of the main emotions present in this situation for the other person. Indicate the exact event or cause for the emotion(s) experienced in this situation:

Anger	Obstacle or injustice	
Surprise	Unexpected Event	
Sadness	A loss	
Fear	Impending Threat	
Disgust	Norms violated	
Happiness	Gain something of value	

Step 5, Move Emotions:

This the last step in the emotional intelligence Blueprint. Determine which Move strategies would be most effective in your situation and how you would implement them. Be as specific as possible—this will increase the likelihood you'll utilize these strategies and do so successfully.

Strategy	Implementation Notes: be specific about how you will implement
Prepare	
Modify Mood	
Reappraise	
Self-talk	
Physiological	
Intervening Moment	
Express a Different Emotion	
Long Term	
Relationships	
Other	

Indicate which Move strategies for the other person would be most effective and how you would implement them. Be as specific as possible as this will increase the likelihood you'll utilize these strategies and do so successfully.

Strategy	Implementation Notes: be specific about how you will implement
Distraction	
Select or Modify Situation	
Change Situation	

Strategy	Implementation Notes: be specific about how you will implement
Emotional Connection	
Match and Validate	
Modulate Tone	
Physiological	
Express Concern	
Intervening Moment	
Other	

Remember, you do not have to select multiple Move strategies! Find the one that you are able to implement and feel will be most effective in the situation.

6. How Did It Go?

It's difficult to objectively evaluate our own skills and outcome. Ideally you would work with a mentor or colleague to debrief on how well it went. If you are unable to do this, then try to answer the "how did it go" question from your perspective but also from the perspective of others involved and how they viewed the outcome.

How satisfied were you with the outcome?	[ ] Not at all [ ] Somewhat [ ] Very [ ] Extremely
How satisfied was the other person with the outcome?	[ ] Not at all [ ] Somewhat [ ] Very [ ] Extremely
Why were all parties extremely satisfied with the outcome?	
If all parties were not extremely satisfied, what would you do differently?	

Build Your Own EI Blueprint—*A Master Class*

Most of our Blueprints involve multiple people, and that makes sense given emotions are often signals about interpersonal relationships. Our Blueprints ask you to reflect on the emotions of the parties involved, but we now want to move to a more in-depth approach to building a Blueprint, one that simultaneously applies the 4 M's to two (or more) people. To do this, we return to an earlier Blueprint (*Pushing My Buttons*) involving a classroom teacher and their student, Oscar. The Blueprint was written from the perspective of the teacher and we recap the situation here again, from the teacher's perspective.

Summary of *Pushing My Buttons*:

	TEACHER	STUDENT (FROM TEACHER'S VIEW)
Step 1, Goal	To begin class without interruption	To embarrass me and make a scene.
Step 2, Map	To be honest, I feel *annoyed*. How could Oscar prioritize breakfast over getting to class on time and being prepared? It's apparent Oscar feels no *shame* or *embarrassment* for disrupting the class and *embarrassing me*.	I am not sure how Oscar feels. I would think he would be *ashamed* or at least *embarrassed* for walking into my classroom late and then storming out.
Step 3, Match	I was justified in terms of being annoyed. Was it helpful? Maybe, maybe not, but being mad was a signal to me and to Oscar that he crossed a line. Maybe it shut me down a little but it was Oscar's behavior which totally ruined my lesson plan for the class.	Ideally, Oscar would have been calmer and more cool-headed so he could reflect on his behavior and not walked out of class.

	TEACHER	STUDENT (FROM TEACHER'S VIEW)
Step 4, Meaning	Oscar and I have a history—and unfortunately, this isn't the first time we clashed. I have every right to feel mad when students disrupt my class by being selfish and prioritizing breakfast over learning.	Obviously Oscar has things going on in his life and he brings his troubles to school with him. I feel badly for him at times but I have a classroom to take care of. He is old enough to take some responsibility for his actions and to plan ahead better. But knowing him, he will settle down for a day or two and then act out once again.
Step 5, Move	I have every right to feel the way I do. I'm the teacher and Oscar disrupted my classroom. I don't see any benefit for modifying my emotions.	Oscar is not a bad kid, but I am not the school social worker. He does these sorts of things every now and then and I assume he will get over this.
Step 6, Outcome	Class was delayed a bit and I will need to deal with Oscar later.	He got the attention he wanted.

Empathy, cognitive empathy, is the ability to take the perspective of another person. Let's look at the *same* situation from the perspective of Oscar, the student.

Here is *Pushing My Buttons* from the point of view of the student:

	STUDENT	TEACHER (STUDENT'S PERSPECTIVE)
Step 1, Goal	Get to school and hope my teacher doesn't hassle me again,	Find something to criticize me about.
Step 2, Map	I knew I was going to be late for class and I was feeling a little *worried*. I was also hungry. Maybe I was a little *embarrassed* to walk in late but then when my teacher flipped out after I was really nice and asked for a pen, I was mad.	As soon as I walked in late, I could see the steam rising from my teacher's head. I am sure she was *angry* with me because this wasn't my first time being late. I have to admit, I liked the *surprise* on her face when I got up and walked out of the classroom.

	STUDENT	TEACHER (STUDENT'S PERSPECTIVE)
Step 3, Match	I was worried about being late and worried I'd get yelled at and being worried was sort of helpful because it got me going. I could've been a lot later, but I was mostly on time.	My teacher not acknowledging me wasn't helpful at all. I really busted my hump to show up on time. She could have at least said hello, or gave me a pen when I asked.
Step 4, Meaning	So maybe sometimes I have a hard time getting to class—especially my first class. I stay up late playing video games and fall asleep at 2 a.m. usually. My parents don't care how much I sleep or oversleep, so I often have to grab something for breakfast. I knew she would make a big deal out of me being late and embarrass me in front of my friends so I was ready for a battle.	I can kind of understand why my teacher got upset with me. She runs a tight ship and always starts class on time. I am not a star student and don't want to be. I think she's given up on me. If she can't get me to learn, I guess she wants me to arrive on time. But, man, did she blow up when I got up to leave class. It's not just my fault, she should have held it together.
Step 5, Move	I had every right to walk out of the classroom. My teacher totally ignored me and I felt disrespected. If I didn't do anything, my friends would have laughed at me and I can't let that happen.	My teacher could have done a lot to keep me in class. First, she could have said hello like I was a real person. She also didn't have to ignore me. She could have just given me a stupid pen and moved on with the class. Instead she yelled at me as I was walking out the door. It was actually she who disrupted the class. I don't care if I ever go to her class again.
Step 6, Outcome	I got into trouble, again, but I have things I am dealing with. And I got to escape from that class.	Her class did not go great and teachers need to control students so this was not a good outcome for her. She's the teacher, not me, but maybe I feel a little bit bad for her.

It may not resemble the plot of Kurosawa's *Rashomon,* but schools are complex communities and it can be difficult to determine root causes of situations or in this case, who is "right." Each person has their own perspective. The idea behind a shared Blueprint approach is to better understand the other person's point of view in order to strengthen the relationship. It's often the case that someone has to mediate, compare notes and arrive at an agreed-upon reality. We chose this Blueprint because it involves a teacher and a student which makes the situation more difficult, politically if nothing else. Ideally, the Blueprint would be used to problem solve and come up with an equitable solution for all parties involved. How could we accomplish this? And without a third party? A series of questions posed to each individual can help to enhance their empathic accuracy:

- Is it possible—possible, not likely, that I am wrong about any of my assumptions?
- If I were the other person, how might I have viewed the situation?
- Assume good intentions and ask, if I were the other person, how might I have felt?
- Assume good intentions and ask, if I were the other person how might I have viewed my actions and intentions?
- Assume good intentions and ask, if I were the other person, how might I have reacted?
- Assume good intentions and ask, if I were the other person, how would they have wanted me to react and respond?

You can also follow the six build your own Blueprint steps, only this time completing the Blueprint as if you are the other person. It's difficult to do well, but simply trying and asking the questions can increase your insight and appreciation of others' complex, inner lives. Let's take a look at how the student and teacher may have answered some of these questions.

Question:	Student: *answering "as-if" they were the teacher*	Teacher: *answering "as-if" they were the student*
Viewed situation	I disrupted class and got in her way	He has a difficult home situation and class can be a safe haven

Question:	Student: *answering "as-if" they were the teacher*	Teacher: *answering "as-if" they were the student*
Felt	She's probably mad at me	Perhaps he is masking his embarrassment by being disruptive
Viewed my actions	My actions looked like I was dissing her	I may have seemed uncaring and rigid when I ignored him
Reacted	When I walked out she yelled at me	I might have walked out too, if my teacher did that to me
Wanted to react and respond	Ignore me, but if not then try to be nice and help me	Apologize for being late and sit down quickly and quietly.

You may quickly see there is no absolute "truth" here. We simply seek to broaden your viewpoints about others and enhance EI skills in order to arrive at a more equitable and just solution when facing difficult challenges.

Concluding Thoughts – and Emotions

Earlier in this book we indicated the real challenge each of us faces is deploying our emotional intelligence skills on a consistent basis, in real-time, at a high level of expertise, under stressful conditions. Our focus for the Blueprints was on challenges you may encounter as an educator. With the suggestions in this book, and our build your own Blueprint template, you can develop approaches to instruction, specific lessons and various interactions to achieve the positive outcomes you desire. Research indicates that more emotionally intelligent educators create positive school climates, have students with greater levels of well-being and even better grades. This is our hope for you – that by developing and leveraging the hard skills of emotional intelligence, you can stay engaged with the work of education, inspire your students to reach their dreams and be a force for positive change.

We hope to inspire you with hope and give you confidence in making a positive difference in the world. We wish you *pleasant* emotions!

PART FOUR

Questions, Answers, Resources

Over the years educators have shared with us their complex challenges, asked some great questions and inquired about what resources are available to continue their EI learning. We've compiled them here and hope you find them useful on your EI journey.

Educator's Key Questions and Issues

We've worked with educators around the world and have heard a lot of questions about emotional intelligence. You may be highly skeptical of EI and its application to you or your school. Or, perhaps you've already bought in on its importance, but wonder about aspects of these programs. Let's tackle some of the questions and issues we've heard over the years.

Is This Another Fad? First, emotional intelligence, as of this book's publication, has a solid thirty-year history of research. It has staying power. Second, EI has been in schools for decades, it's not the latest flavor.

I Don't Have Time for This! We realize you have enough to do without adding another module or another lesson to your day. Our focus is on sharpening your skills which you can then apply in the moment. We are not asking for more of your time, we are asking you to spend some of that time differently.

I Can't Ask Teachers or Students "how are you feeling?" Then ask another question. We recognize your culture may not allow such a direct question. Instead, come up with your own way of asking, perhaps focusing on tone, or modeling this yourself. For example, when asked "how are you?" you might respond "good, but a bit worried about my parent meeting and not sure how to prepare for it." We've all worked with educators and have been impressed with ways to ask the "how are you?" question while not violating the behavioral norms of their schools and cultures. However you figure it out, remember that mapping feelings accurately is an essential aspect of developing emotional intelligence.

We Believe in 'Strong Leadership', Not Emotional Leadership. We hear this one a lot, especially outside the U.S. Strong leaders instill a sense of urgency and pride in their organization. Urgency is generated from anxiety (an emotion) and pride (a strong emotion). Strong leaders know this and EI can underpin strong leadership. EI leaders are not sobbing at meetings and talking about feelings all the time. They leverage and harness the power of emotions to achieve goals. The key is you need to tap into the power of emotions with great sophistication.

We've Done EI Before. You may have run a teacher workshop on EI but our guess is you have not trained on the ability model where emotions are data and helpful in decision making. Consider a hard-skills approach to EI with the use of the Blueprint and the four abilities of emotional intelligence.

We've Already Done RULER Training. If you have received RULER training, this book will seem familiar and can help you implement the program content. As we've noted, we've changed the Mood Meter into the Mood Map but this book should complement your RULER training quite nicely. The official training is very well done and extremely comprehensive whereas our book provides a helpful and much more basic overview. Please note that RULER training does not endorse our book.

Where Is Your Proof? As you know, CASEL has a set of approved programs with evidence of efficacy. Our book is not CASEL-approved and our specific exercises have not been included in a controlled study. They are based on the ability model of emotional intelligence with decades of research behind it, the same model RULER is based on. However, our book has not been reviewed or endorsed by CASEL.

These Blueprints Seem Pretty Easy. They are—once you lay out the challenge and focus on the underlying emotional causes. The challenge for you is to address problems in the moment, or even better, to use a structured approach to emotion-based problem solving to avoid creating a problem in the first place. Each Blueprint is easy on its own, but we find it takes a lot of skill as well as a great deal of effort to consistently and effectively leverage EI in every critical situation.

Are You Saying Anger is Helpful? There are reasons to be angry as we face injustice and inequities. Anger can fuel change but acting angrily is a bad idea. Anger is a corrosive and dangerous emotion. You need highly-advanced emotion management skills to be an effective manager of anger. Nothing in this book gives you permission to be a jerk! You can only harness the power of anger for social justice if you are a master of emotions, and frankly, few of us are. Consider the examples of people like Rosa Parks, Dr. King or Mahatma Gandhi to illustrate how hard and rare it is to leverage the power of anger in the service of a larger cause.

Can EI Be Used Negatively? Can you use these skills to manipulate people? Unfortunately, perhaps you can and that concerns us. Properly used, these skills result in positive outcomes for everyone, but in the wrong hands, it is possible to wreak havoc on the lives of people. But it is unlikely, and there are several reasons for this. For example, some data exist to suggest that people who score high in EI, score lower on Machiavellianism. People with high EI have better long-term quality relationships which means they are not using their abilities for evil purposes. Empathy plays a role here as well; if I feel your pain I will not intentionally harm you. At the same time, there are a few studies that people high on emotion management and Machiavellianism can and do use their ability to manipulate people.

I Find It Hard to Generate Positive Emotions, Is That a Problem? Few of us can process all emotions equally well. Some people tend to live in the "middle" of the Mood Map and don't experience strong emotions or swings. But if you find it difficult to generate positive emotions and find yourself feeling sad much of the time, you should certainly consult a professional. The American Psychological Association has a search function on its website at http://www.apa.org/helpcenter/.

Should I Always Try to Work It Out Using EI Skills? The approach we take in this book is learning how to use your emotions to achieve your goals and how to use them in constructive ways. There may be times when either the Blueprint approach does not work or the situation is serious enough to refer to the building principal, superintendent's office or social worker.

SOME RESOURCES

Measuring Emotional Intelligence—There are three ways to measure an ability: you can ask people to provide their own estimate, you can ask others to estimate a person's ability or you can give the person an ability test. Once you select the overall method, you then need to develop test items that measure EI according to how you define EI. For us, the best way to measure EI is with an ability test where items measure Perceive (Map), Facilitate (or often labeled Use, in this book we call it Match), Understand (Meaning) and Manage (Move). The Mayer, Salovey, Caruso Emotional Intelligence Test (MSCEIT) does just this. It's a bit unusual but it often provides interesting insights into your EI skills. The MSCEIT – Youth Research Version is available for testing of students from 10 to 17 years of age.

Books—We have other books on EI, *The Emotionally Intelligent Manager* and *A Leader's Guide to Solving Challenges with Emotional Intelligence,* but there are many other books as well, although they view EI differently than we do. The book that catapulted the concept into the public sphere is Goleman's *Emotional Intelligence.* While Goleman stretched the concept of EI, his book is well written.

Articles and Websites—The best start is CASEL (casel.org) for resources and articles. Websites on EI abound and here is a plug for our sites: eiteacher.org, ltrleadership.com and eiskillsgroup.com. Six Seconds has a different approach and terrific resources so check them out (6seconds.org). For general information on EI see Jack Mayer's site at http://www.mypages.unh.edu/jdmayer. Some articles of interest include these:

MacCann, C., et.al. (2019). Emotional Intelligence Predicts Academic Performance: A Meta-Analysis. Psychological Bulletin, 146, 150-186.

MacCann, C., Joseph, D., Newman, D., Roberts, R. (2014). Emotional Intelligence Is a Second-Stratum Factor of Intelligence: Evidence From Hierarchical and Bifactor Models. Emotion, 14(2), 358-374.

Mayer, J. D., Caruso, D. R., & Salovey, P. (2016). The ability model of emotional intelligence: Principles and updates. Emotion Review, 8, 1-11.

Mayer, J. D., & Salovey, P. (1997). What is emotional intelligence? In D. J. Sluyter (Ed.), Emotional development and emotional intelligence: Educational implications. (pp. 3-34). New York, NY US: Basic Books.

If you are interested in exploring some of the research behind the concepts in our book, consider starting with some of these articles. As you explore the field, do take care to read the full article in order to understand how the researcher is defining and measuring emotional intelligence.

ABOUT THE AUTHORS

David R. Caruso, Ph.D. David is the co-founder of *Emotional Intelligence (EI) Skills Group.* In addition, he is a research affiliate at the Yale Center for Emotional Intelligence and the Senior Advisor to the Dean of Yale College. David is the co-author of the Mayer, Salovey, Caruso Emotional Intelligence Test (MSCEIT). He and  colleague Peter Salovey wrote *The Emotionally Intelligent Manager.* David is a co-author of *The Anchors of Emotional Intelligence* RULER program (Brackett, Caruso & Stern) and is the developer of the "Mood Meter" and EI "Blueprint." David has published numerous articles – peer reviewed journal articles, reviews and chapters—on emotional intelligence. He has trained thousands of people around the world. His interest in education goes back more than 40 years after he dropped out of college and took a series of jobs working in various educational programs. He was a teacher's assistant in one of the first public school programs for multiply-handicapped, severely mentally retarded children in Maine. He returned to college as a way to continue this work, albeit in a different manner. After college, he earned his Ph.D. in psychology from Case Western Reserve University and was awarded a two-year postdoctoral fellowship in psychology at Yale University where he worked with Ed Zigler (one of the founders of Project Head Start) and Bob Sternberg (intelligence researcher). Contact: david@eiskills.com

Lisa T. Rees, PCC, MPA Lisa is an experienced leader, coach and instructor with the U.S. Citizenship and Immigration Services (USCIS). Having worked over three decades for USCIS (legacy Immigration and Naturalization Service), Lisa led teams in implementing financial systems and cost efficiencies throughout her agency before switching career fields to become a certi-

fied leadership coach in 2015. Lisa has an A.S. in Accounting and a B.S. in Management from Champlain College and her Master in Public Administration from Norwich University. Lisa is certified in the MSCEIT, as well as certified in Appreciative Inquiry (AI) and numerous leadership assessment tools. Lisa is a strategic partner with the David L. Cooperrider Center of Appreciative Inquiry and teaches EI and AI at the Naval Postgraduate School in Monterey, CA. In addition to working for USCIS, Lisa has her own leadership consulting practice, LTR Leadership, where she provides consulting, facilitates workshops and coaches executives and their teams using EI and AI as the foundation for her practice. This is Lisa's second book and she has written several journal articles on EI and AI. Contact: lisa@ltrleadership.com.

David Adams, M.Ed. David Adams is the Director of Social-Emotional Learning at The Urban Assembly. He previously served as the Social-Emotional Learning Coordinator for District 75 in New York City, where he shaped the District's approach to social and emotional development for students with severe cogni-

tive and behavioral challenges. He has worked internationally in schools in England, standing up and evaluating programs of positive behavioral supports and social-emotional learning as a research intern at Yale University's Health, Emotion and Behavior Lab, and published multiple academic papers around the relationship of social-emotional competence, and student academic and behavioral outcomes. David serves on the Board of Directors of CASEL and served on the Council of Distinguished Educators of the Aspen Institute's National Commission of Social, Emotional and Academic Development (NCSEAD), and is married with two children. He is a Civil Affairs Officer in the Army Reserve and holds M.Ed. in Educational Psychology from Fordham University. Contact: dadams@urbanassembly.org.

ACKNOWLEDGEMENTS
AND THANK-YOUS

Emotions form the basis of relationships, and, as it turns out, relationships created emotional intelligence. John (Jack) Mayer and David were fellow grad students in their Ph.D. program at Case Western Reserve University. David met Peter Salovey when Peter was a grad student at Yale where David was a postdoctoral fellow in psychology. Jack and Peter met separately at emotions conferences and found they had many things in common. From their informal discussions came their theory of emotional intelligence. This book is based on the work of Jack and Peter but they have neither reviewed nor approved of the content. We are grateful to Adam Robinson of Good Book Developers for turning our vision from a document into a book and to James S. (Jim) Norton for his editing.

David Caruso: I am truly grateful for Peter and Jack's willingness to work with me on their ability model of EI. My wife, Nancie (a child clinical psychologist), my three children, my son-in-law, my daughter-in-law and my grandchildren continue to improve my EI skills.

Lisa Rees: When I was studying for my Master in Public Administration I kept reading about the importance of emotionally intelligent leadership. I was so intrigued, I contacted David Caruso about getting certified in EI. His mentorship, friendship, advice and faith in me gave me the courage to share EI in the federal workplace and co-author two books with him. I can't thank him enough for the opportunity to share my passion for EI with the world. I also have to thank my amazing husband, Grant. His love, support and encouragement, to go after my dreams, has allowed me to soar to places I didn't think possible.

David Adams: I could not co-author a book about emotional intelligence without taking this opportunity to thank my wife Tomeeka. Her grace and diligence impress me every day, and without her I could not be the husband, father, officer and educator that I aspire to be.

Many thanks,
David R. Caruso New Haven, Connecticut
Lisa T. Rees Burlington, Vermont
David Adams New York City, New York

Made in the USA
Coppell, TX
29 July 2021